Woodland Litter Critters ABC

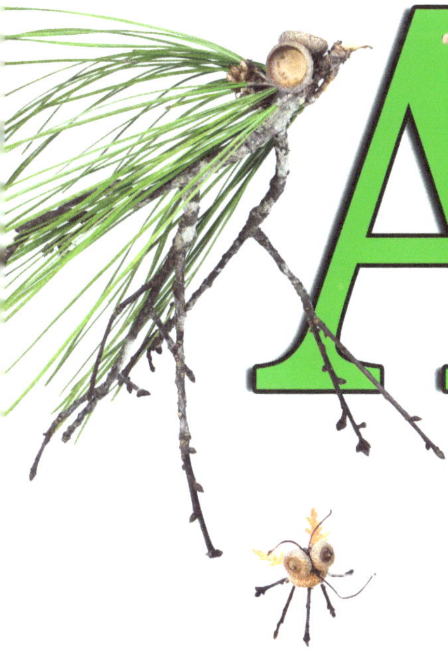

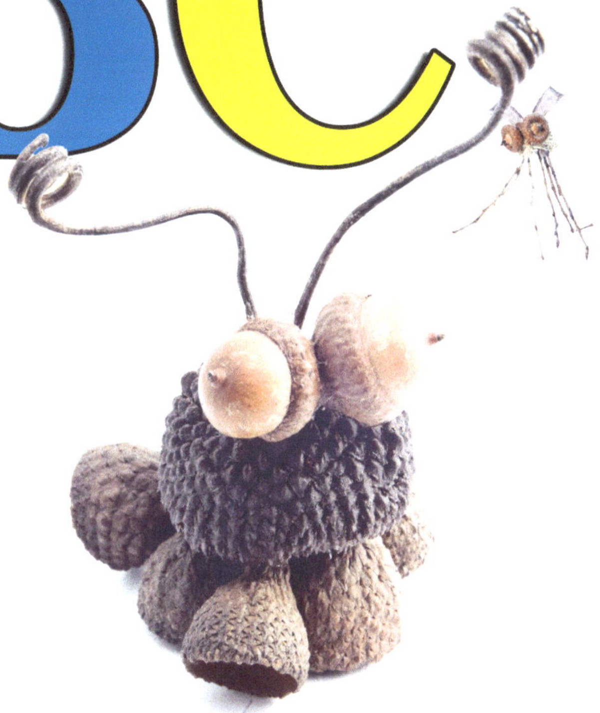

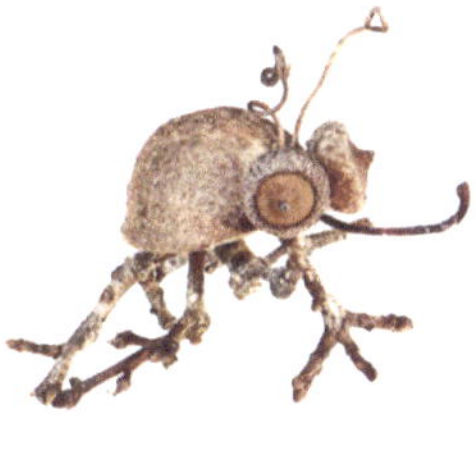

Story and Critters by
Patience Mason

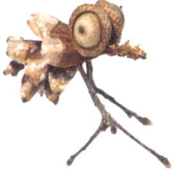

Illustrated by
Robert Mason

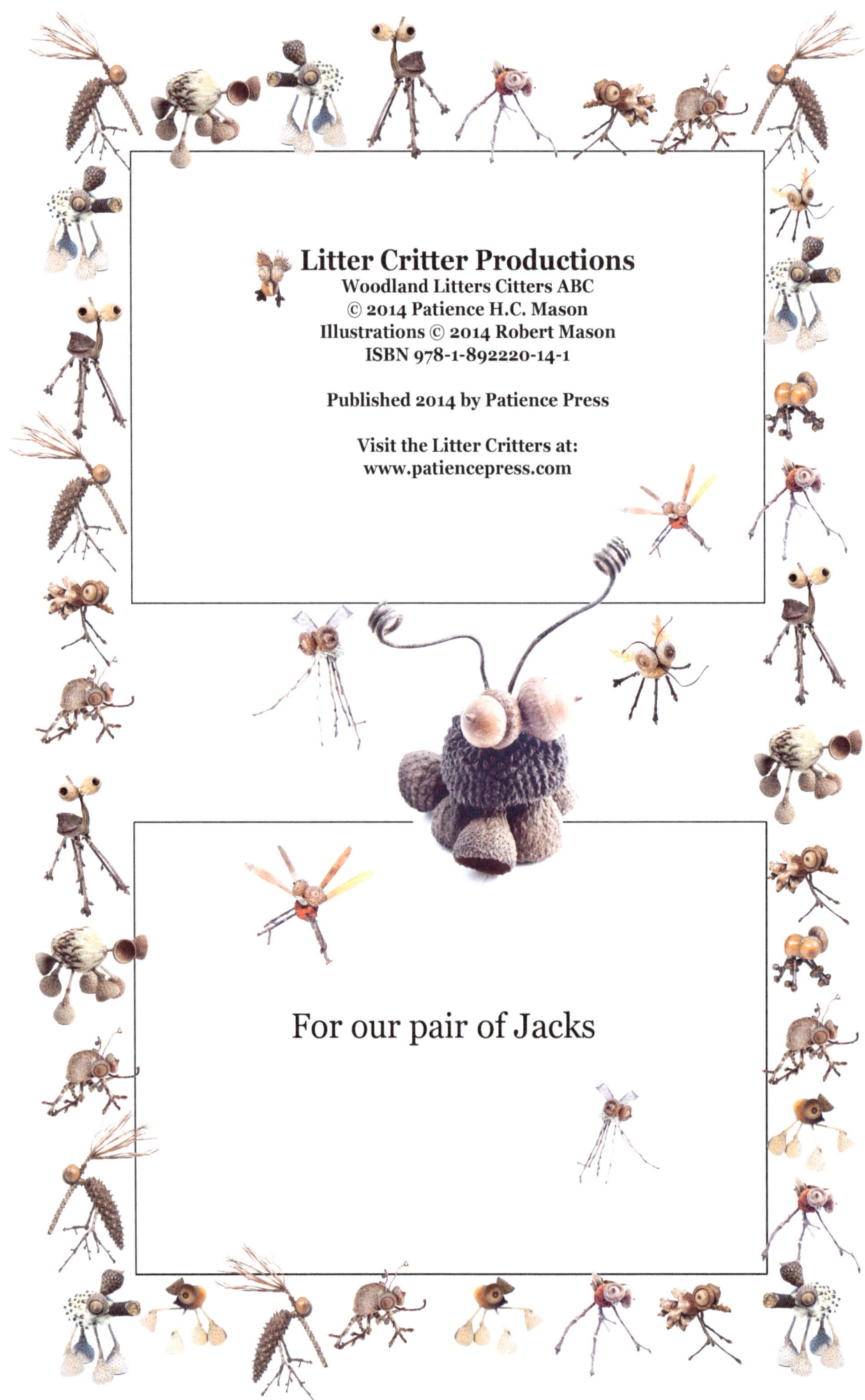

Litter Critter Productions
Woodland Litters Citters ABC
© 2014 Patience H.C. Mason
Illustrations © 2014 Robert Mason
ISBN 978-1-892220-14-1

Published 2014 by Patience Press

Visit the Litter Critters at:
www.patiencepress.com

For our pair of Jacks

Near the shady river at the end of the day,

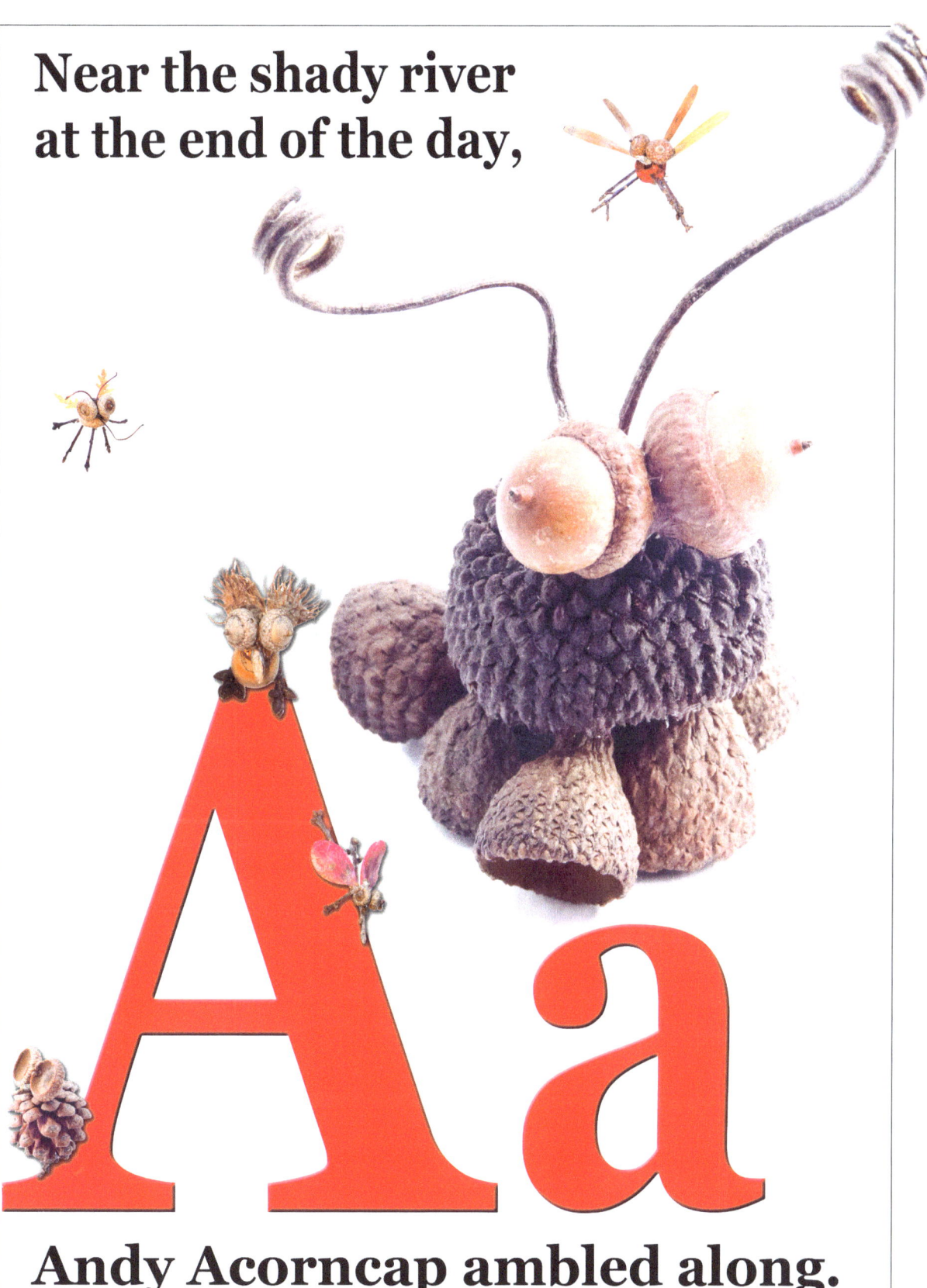

Aa

Andy Acorncap ambled along.

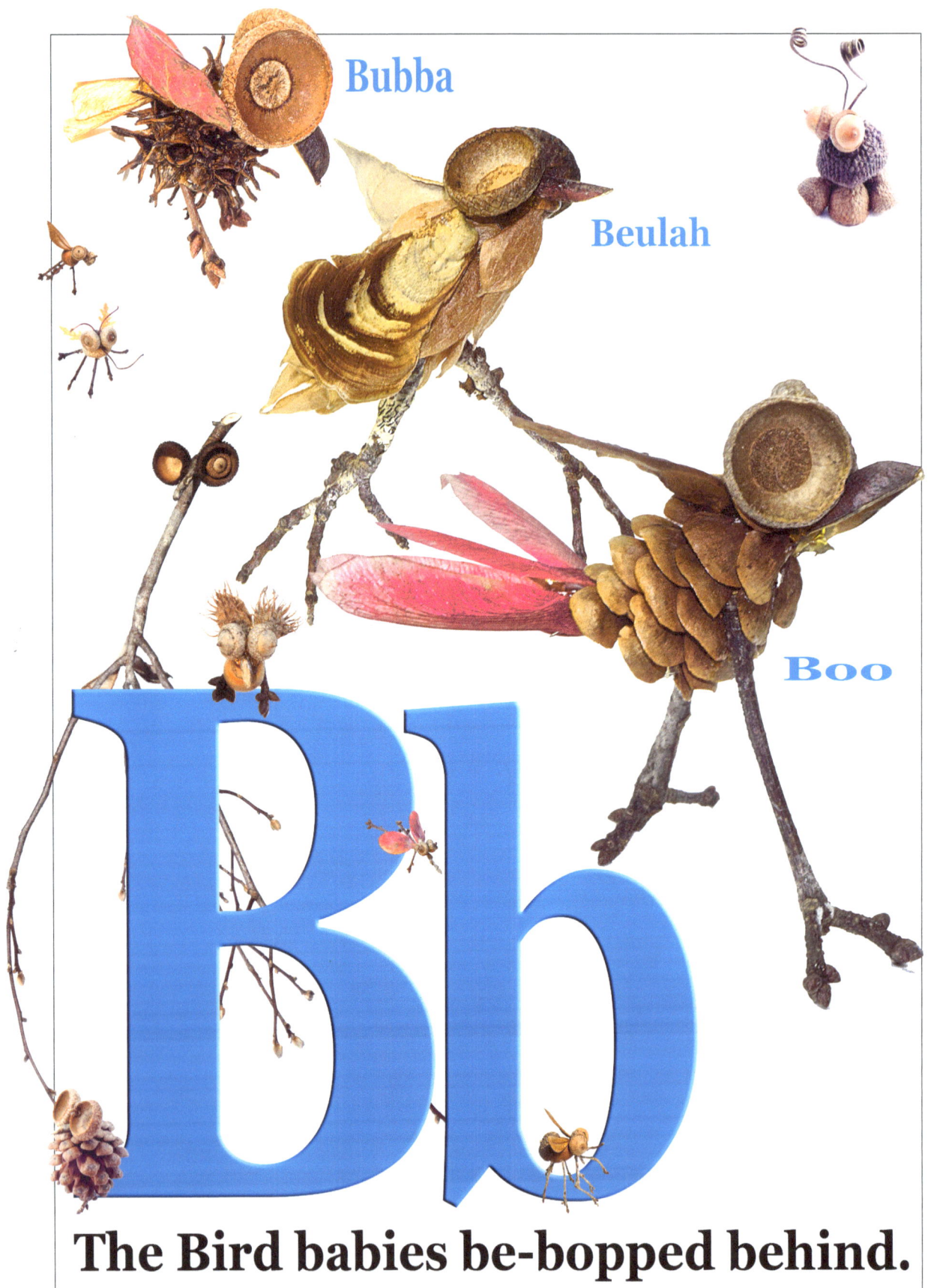

The Bird babies be-bopped behind.

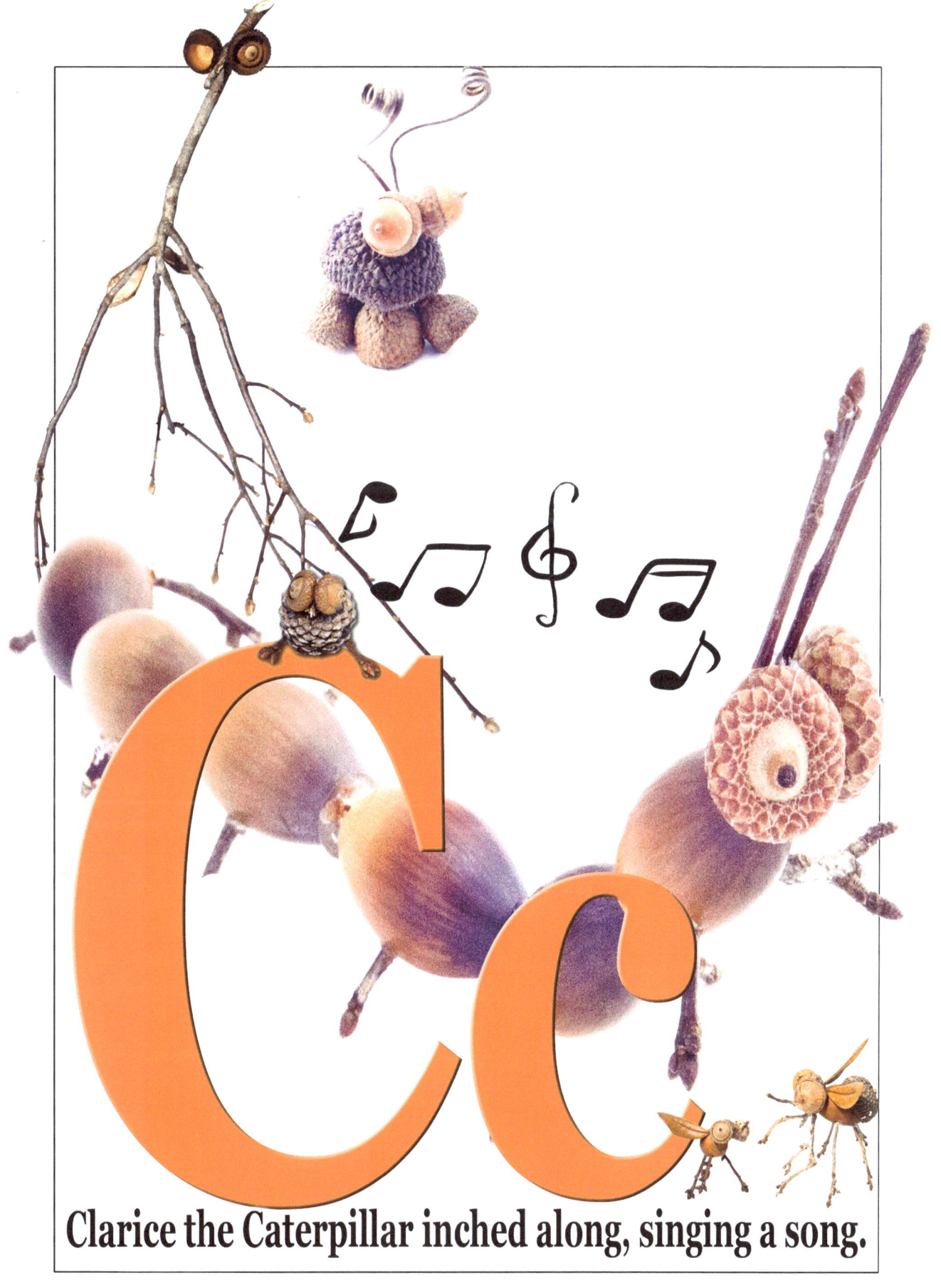

Clarice the Caterpillar inched along, singing a song.

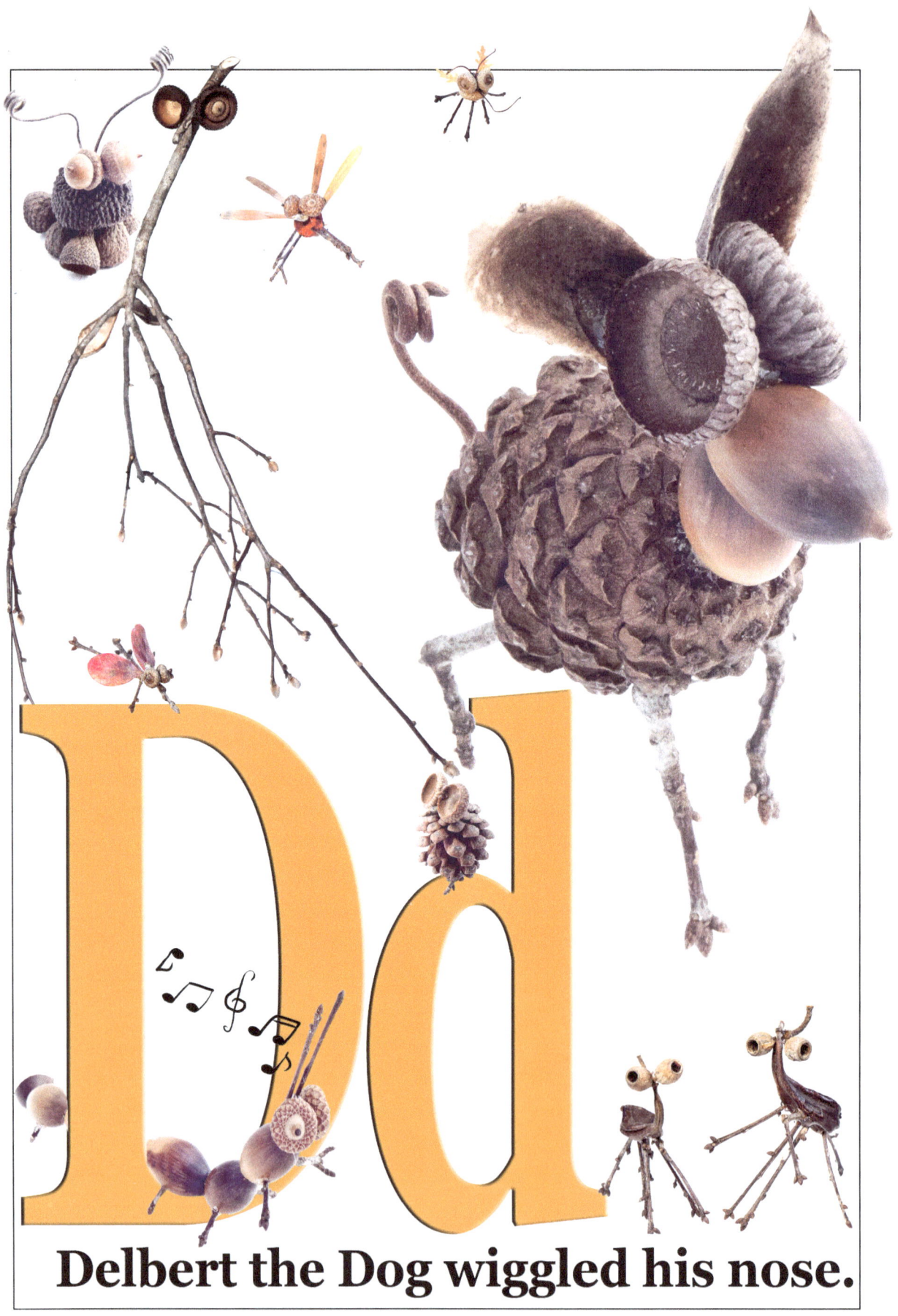

Delbert the Dog wiggled his nose.

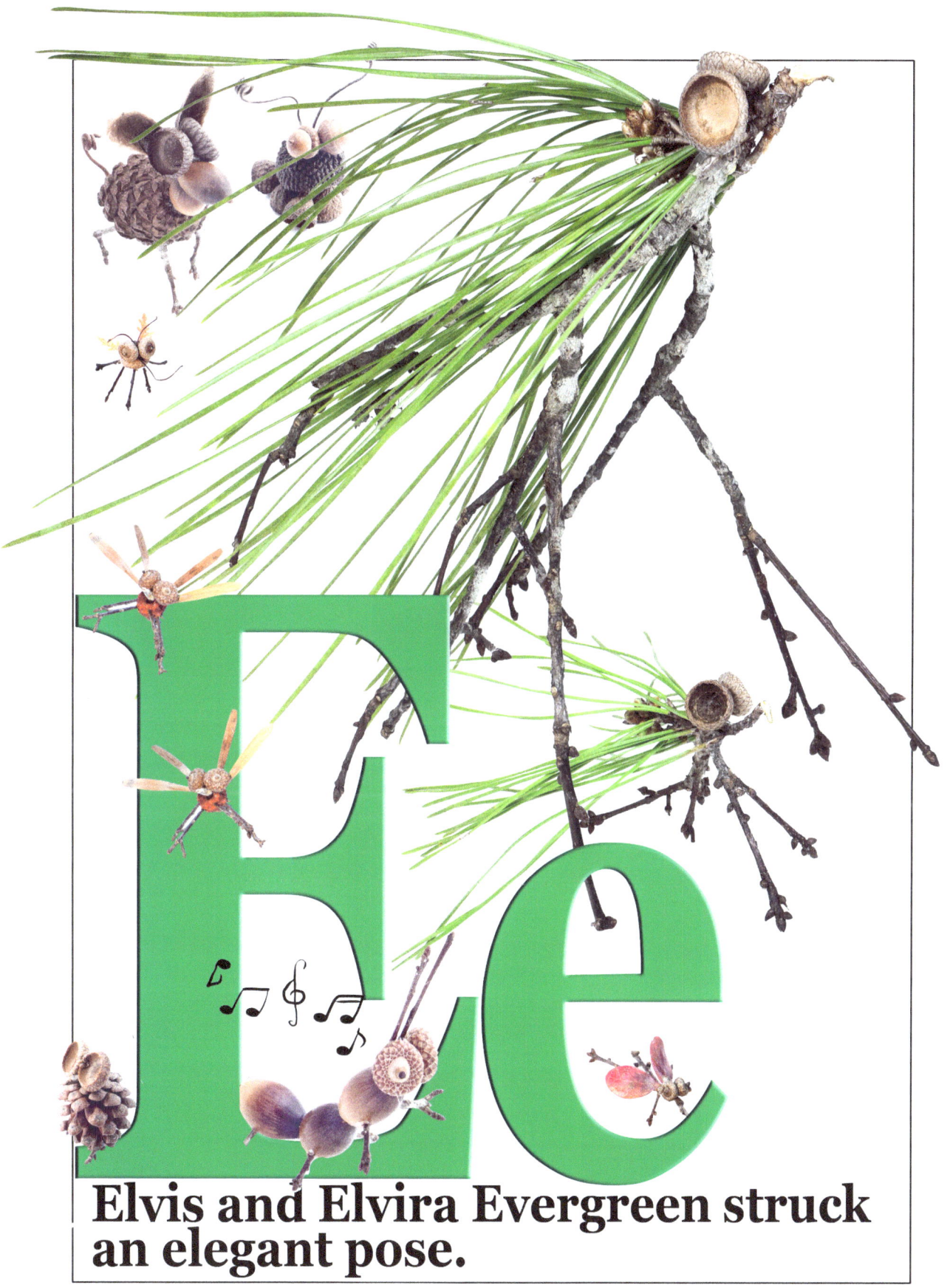

Elvis and Elvira Evergreen struck an elegant pose.

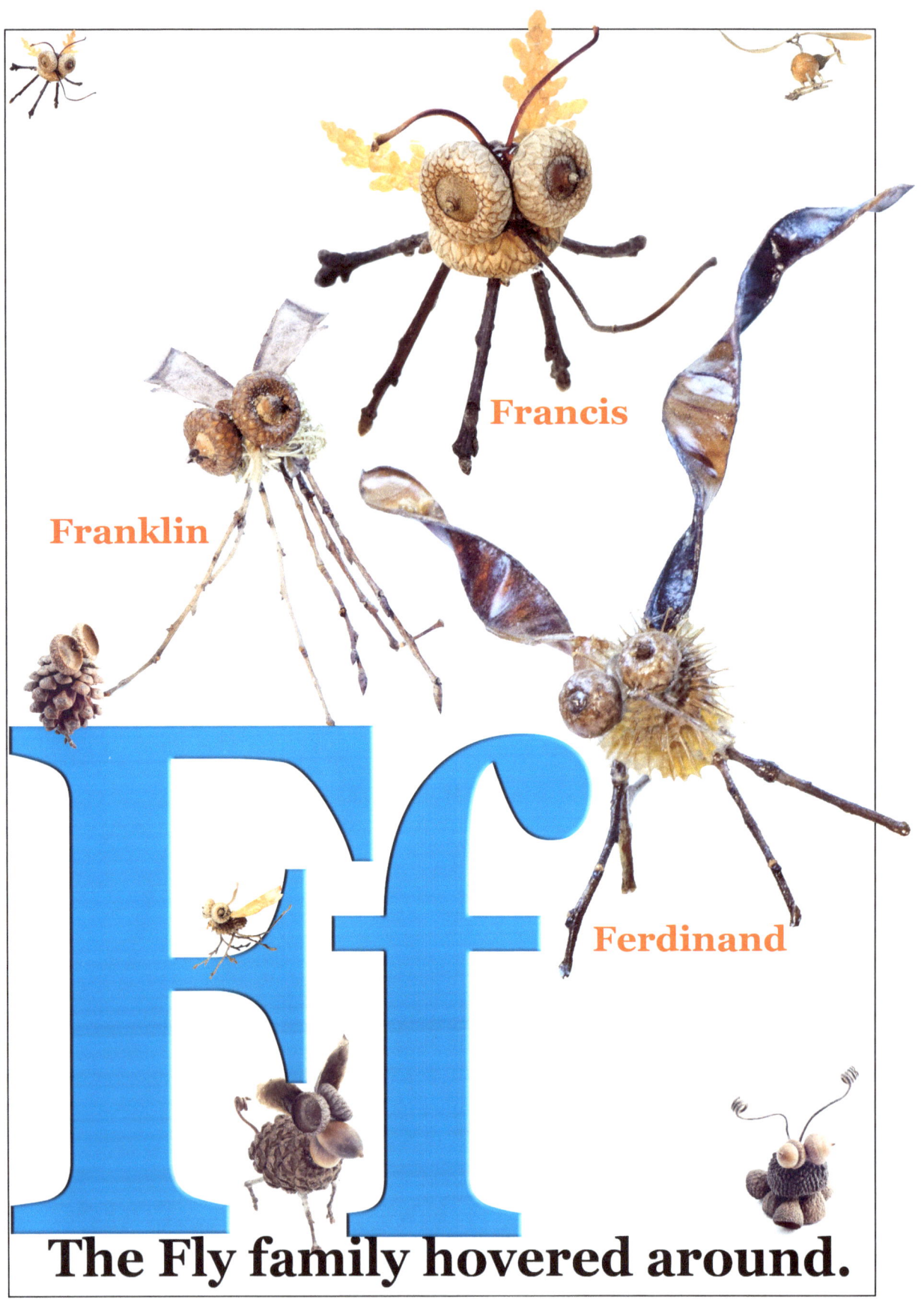

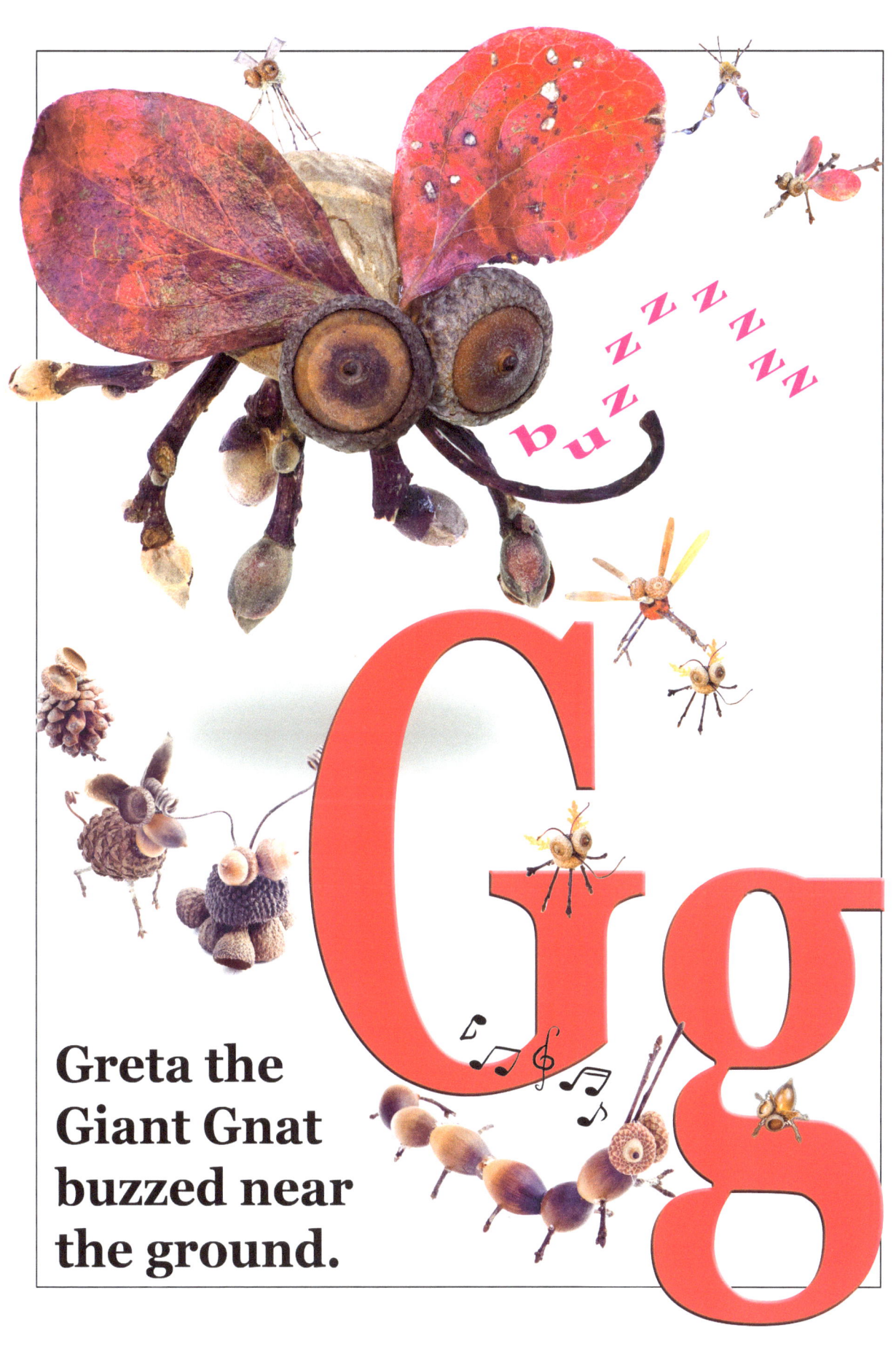

Greta the Giant Gnat buzzed near the ground.

Hh

Hieronymus and Harriet Hickorynut showed up together.

ii

Nice day! *Very sunny!*

Isabella and Ivan Iris-pod talked about the weather.

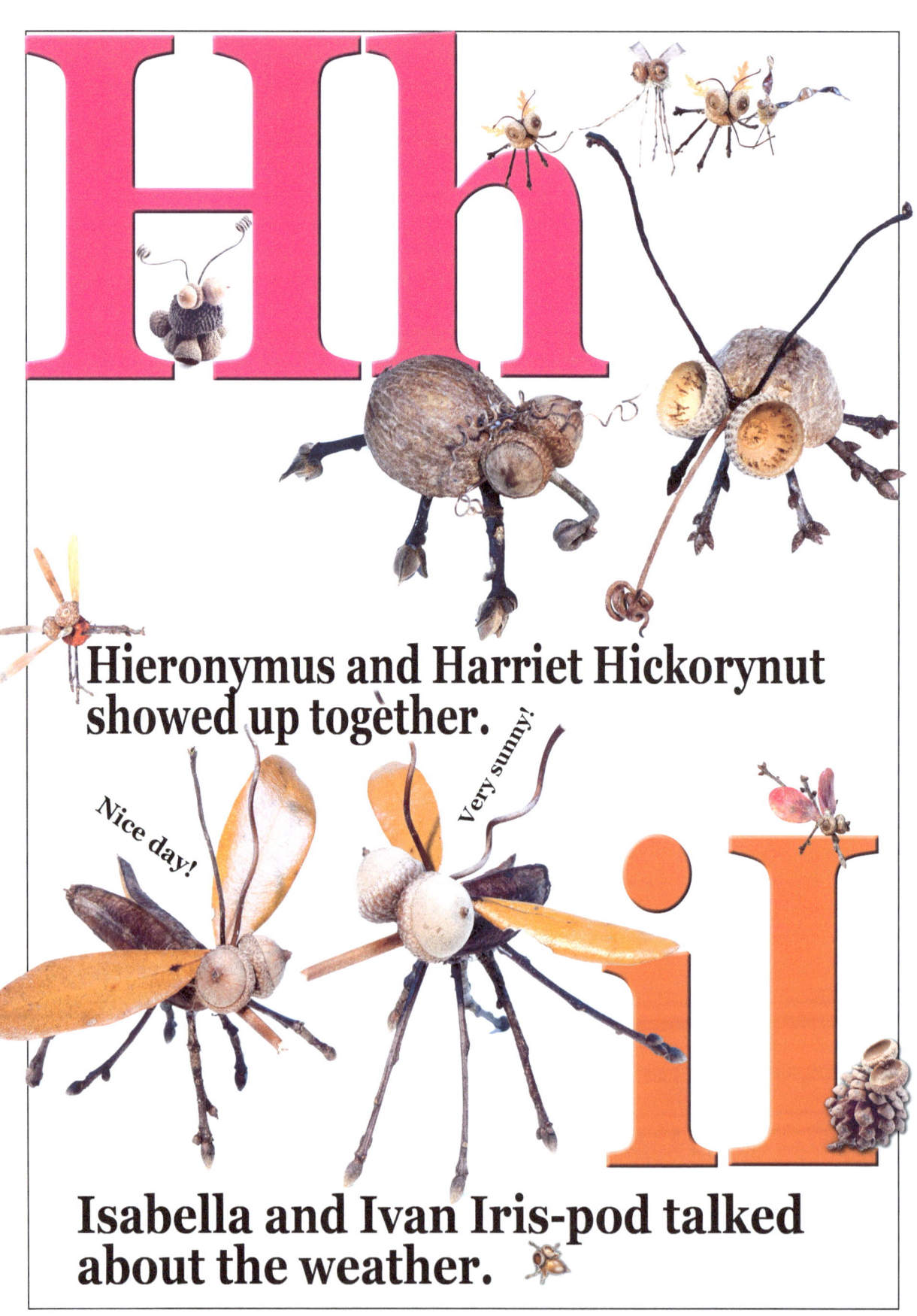

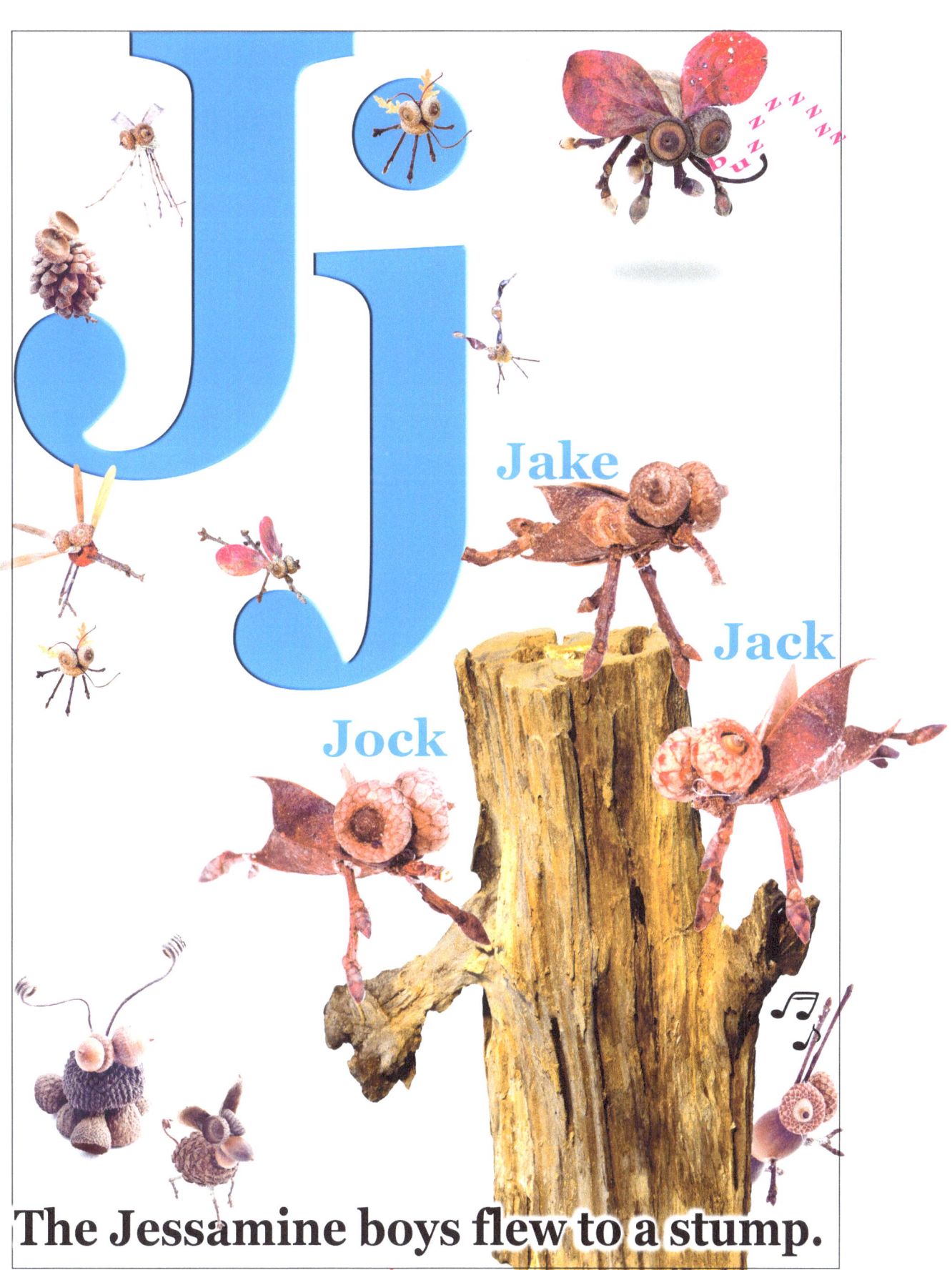

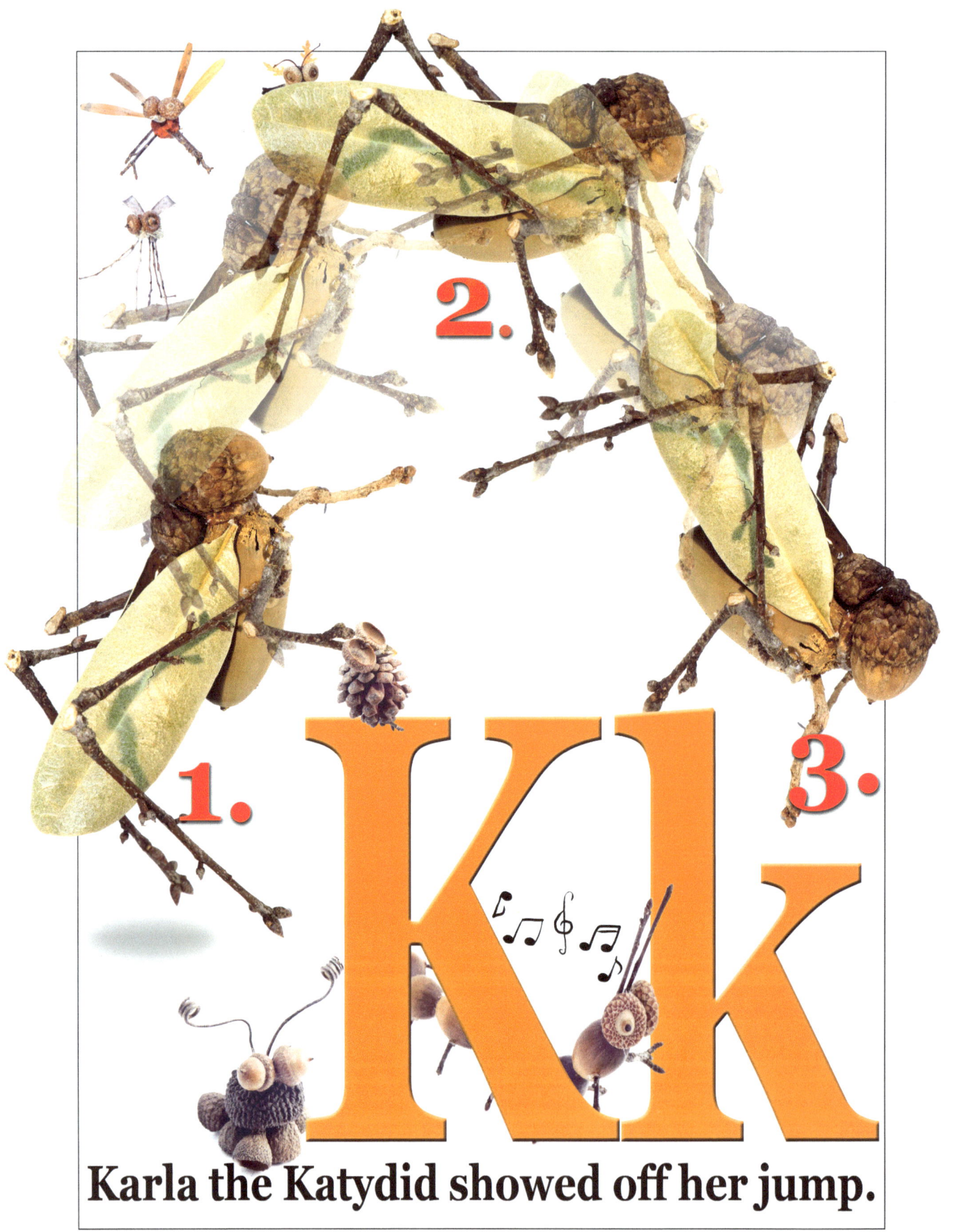

Karla the Katydid showed off her jump.

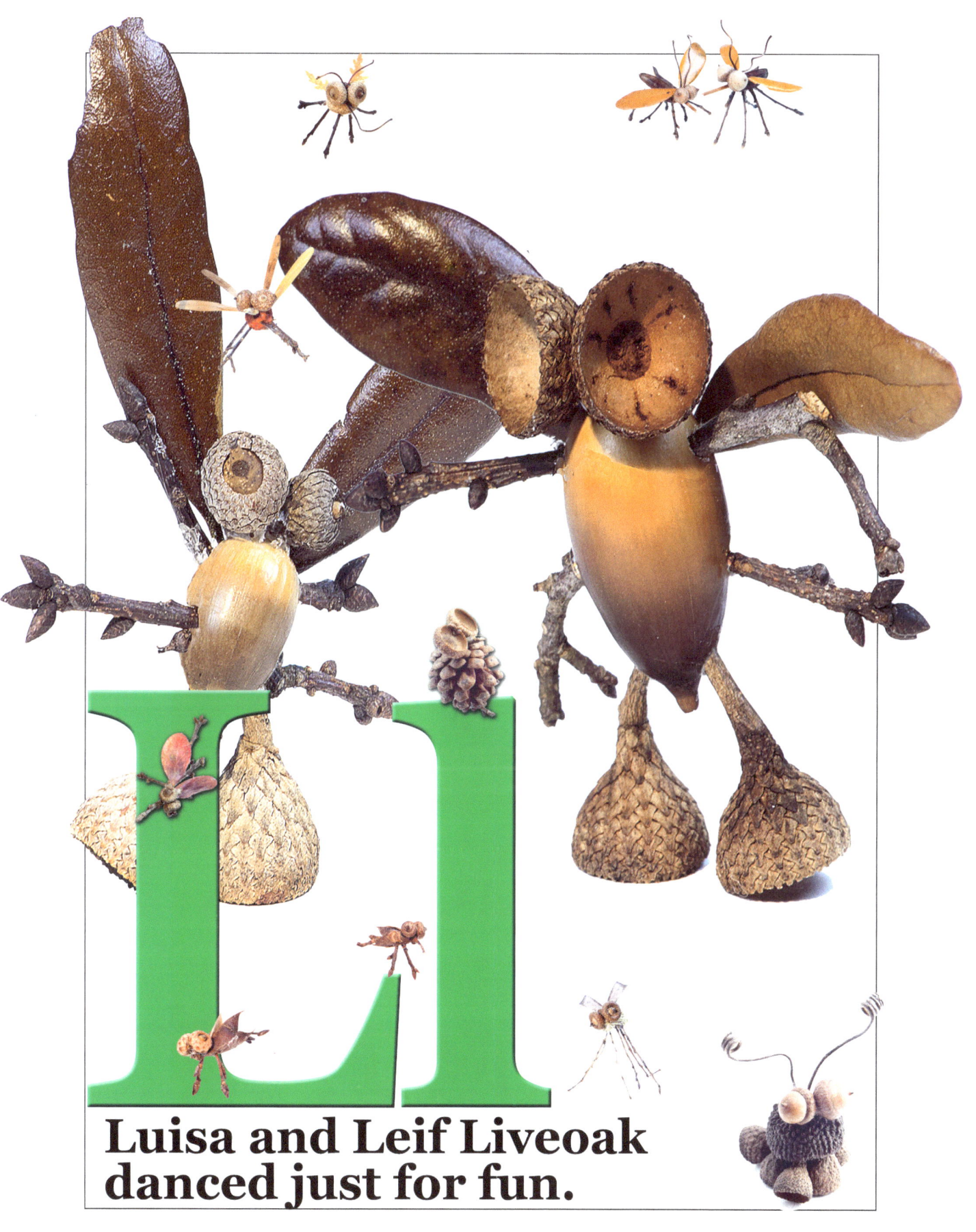

Luisa and Leif Liveoak danced just for fun.

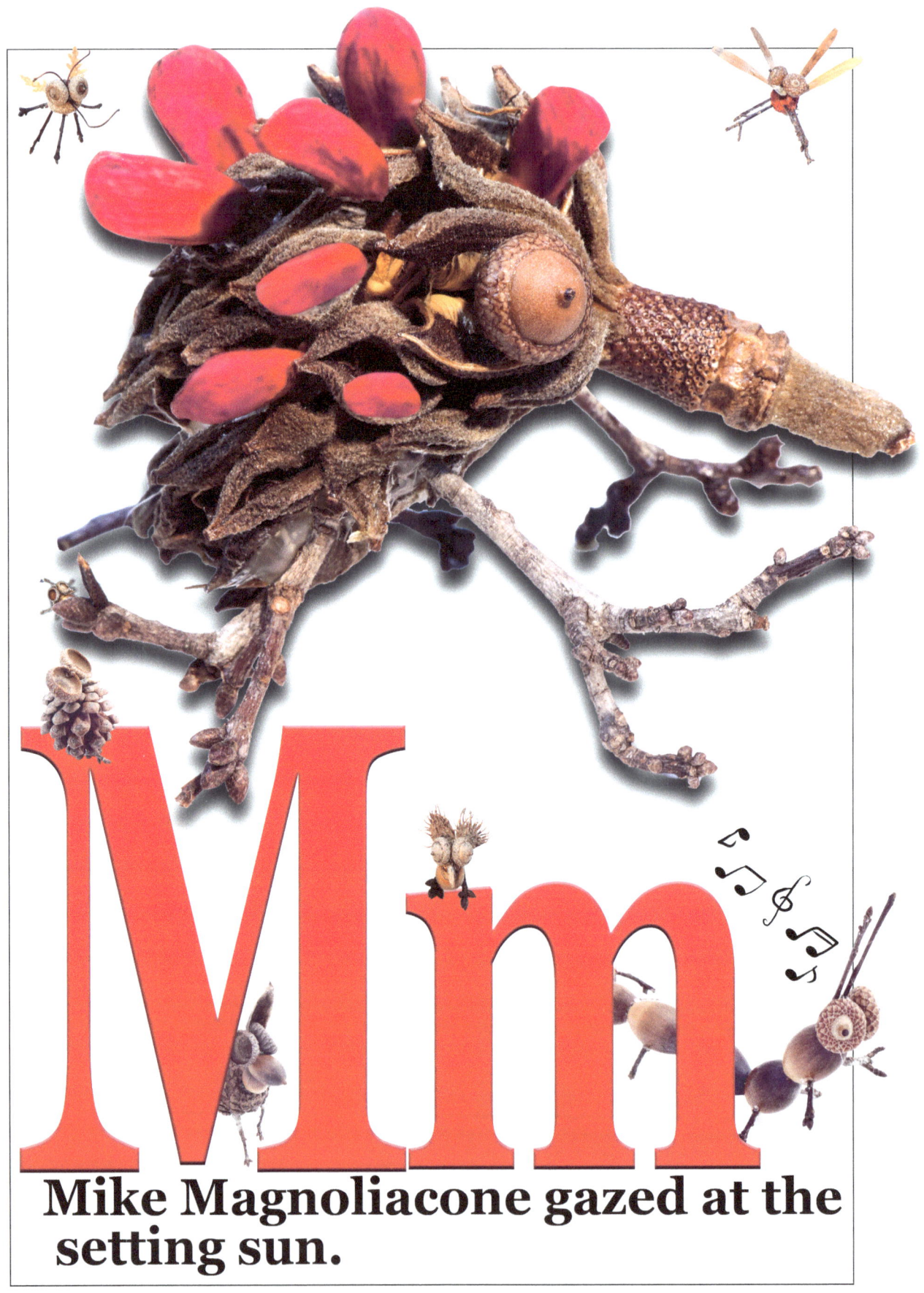

Mike Magnoliacone gazed at the setting sun.

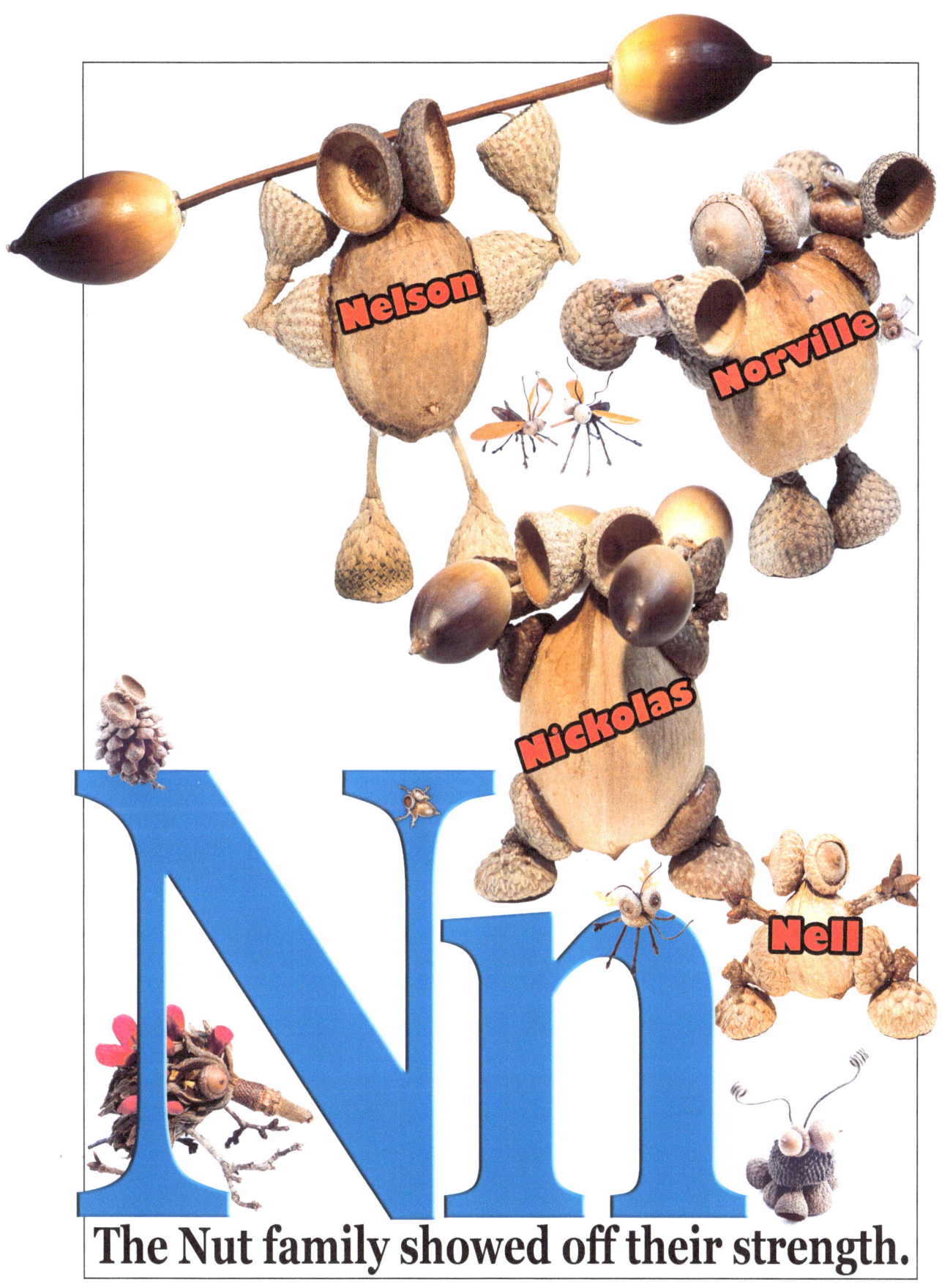

The Nut family showed off their strength.

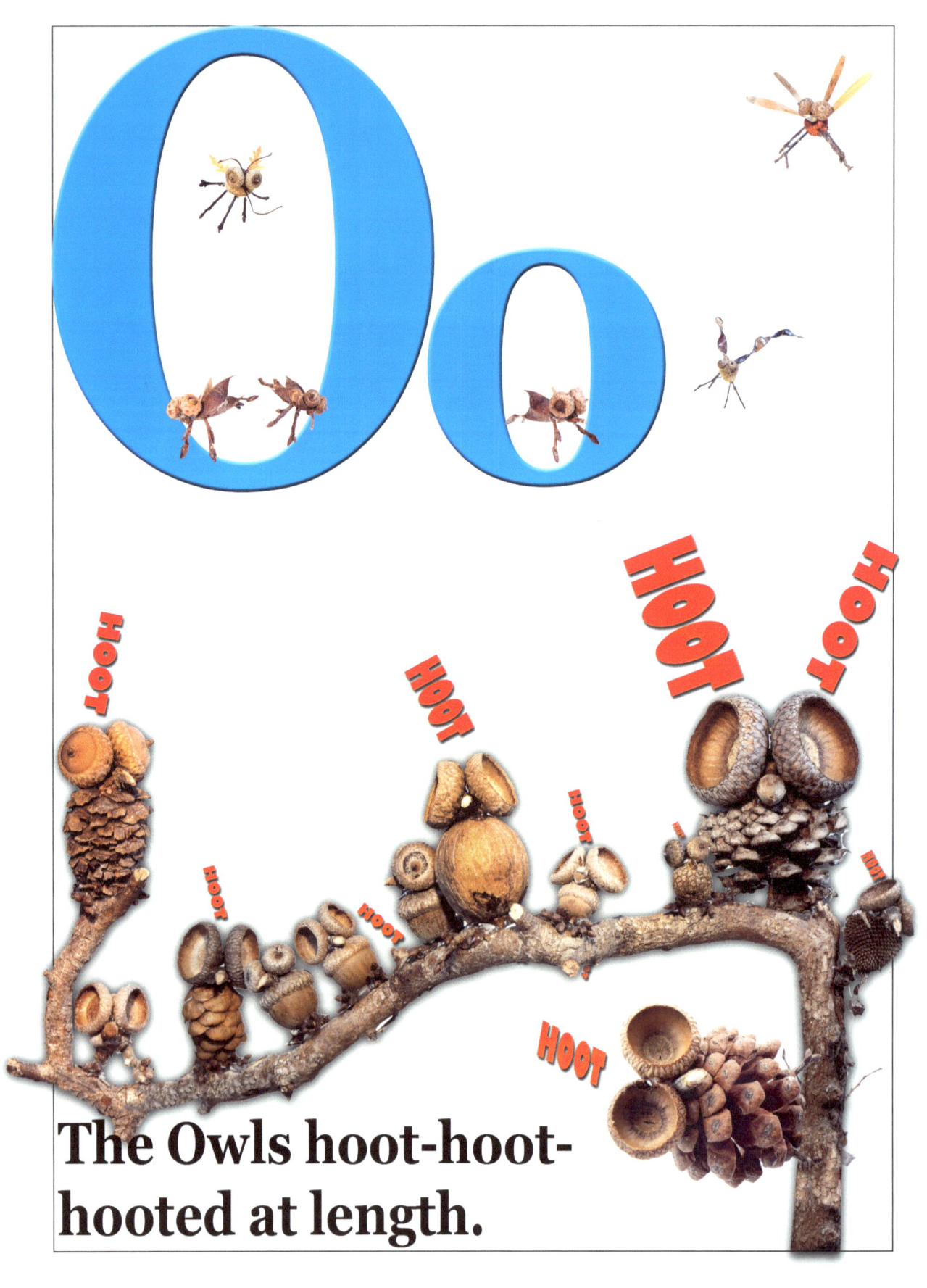

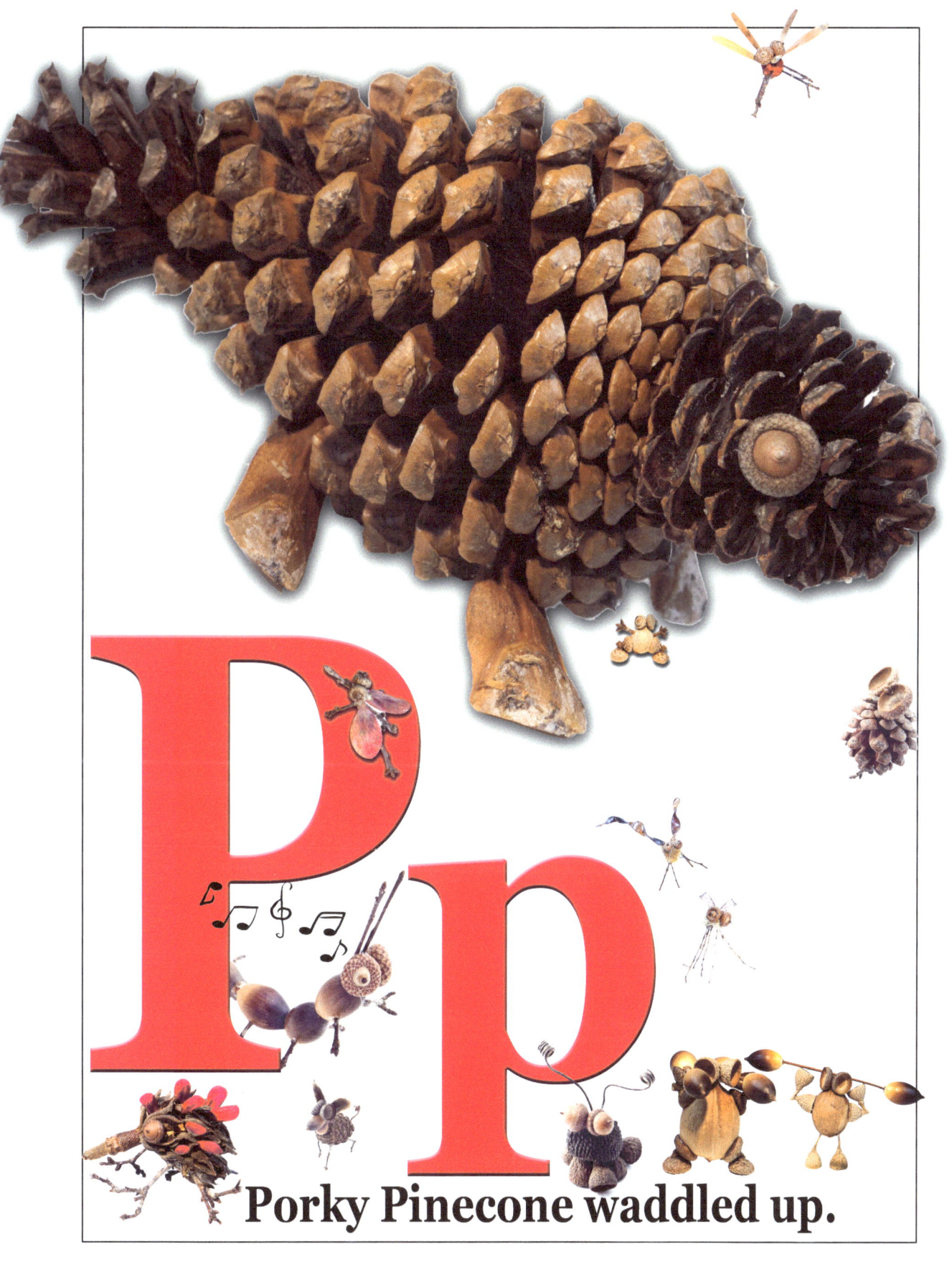

Porky Pinecone waddled up.

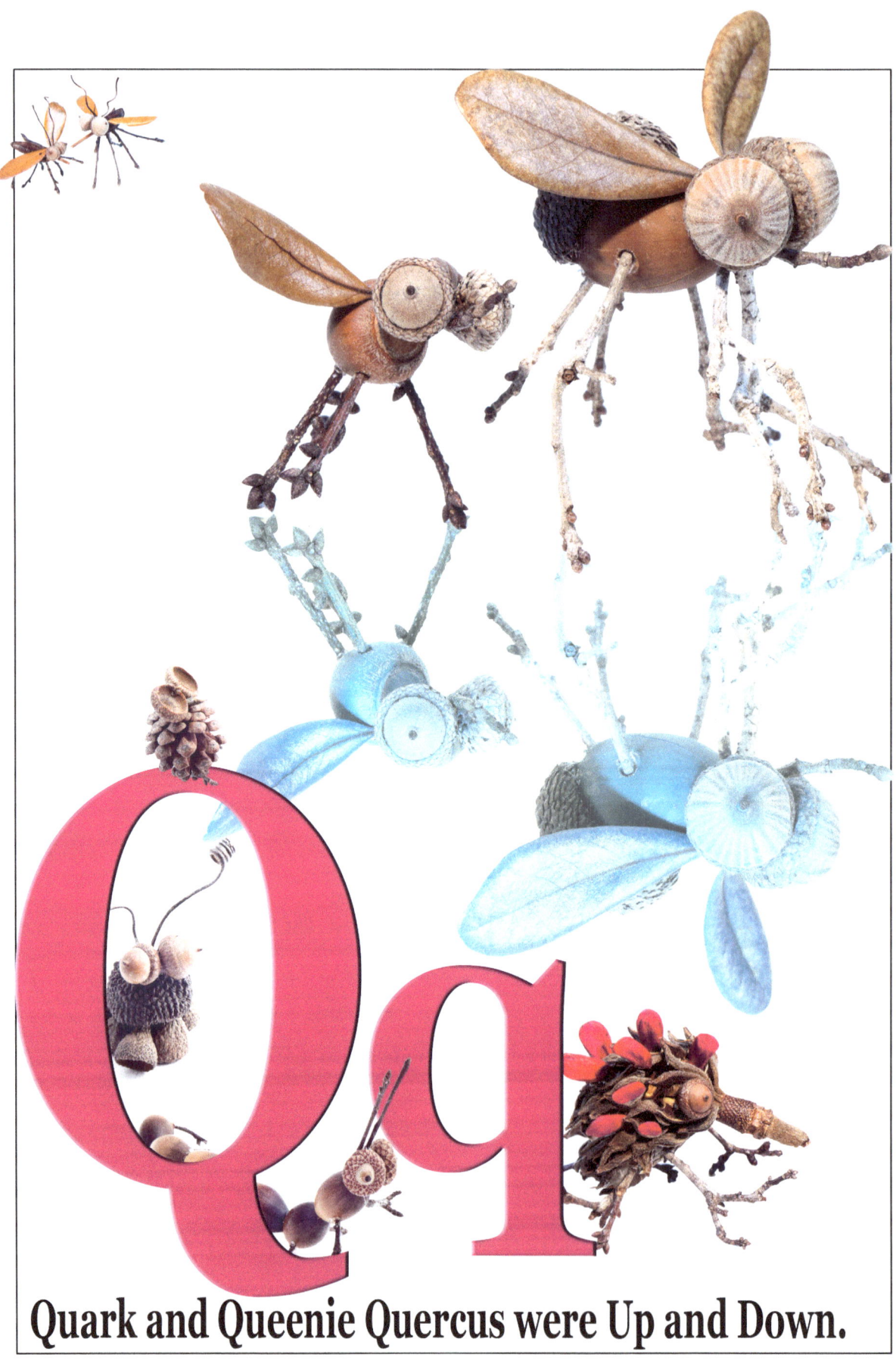

Quark and Queenie Quercus were Up and Down.

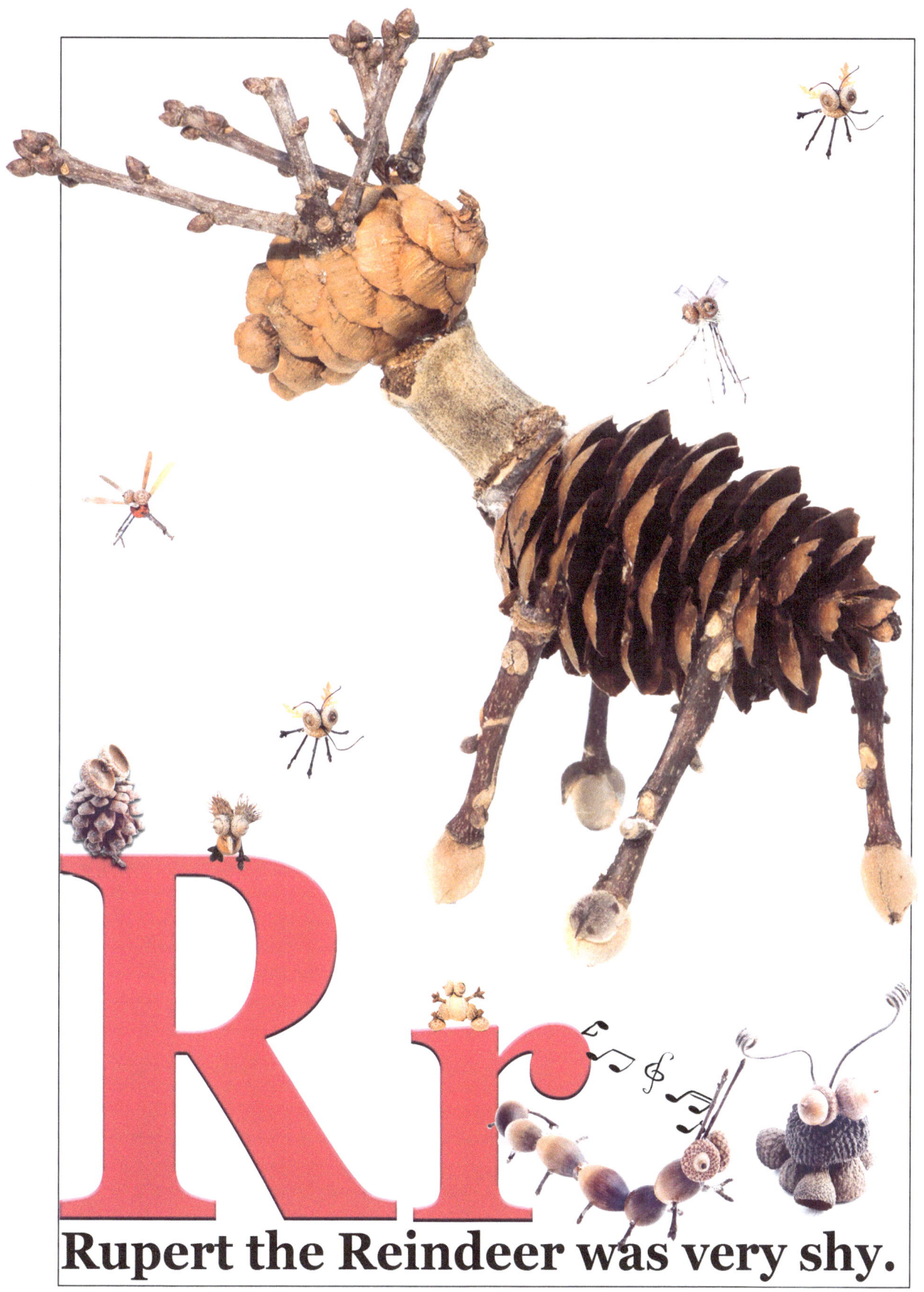

Rupert the Reindeer was very shy.

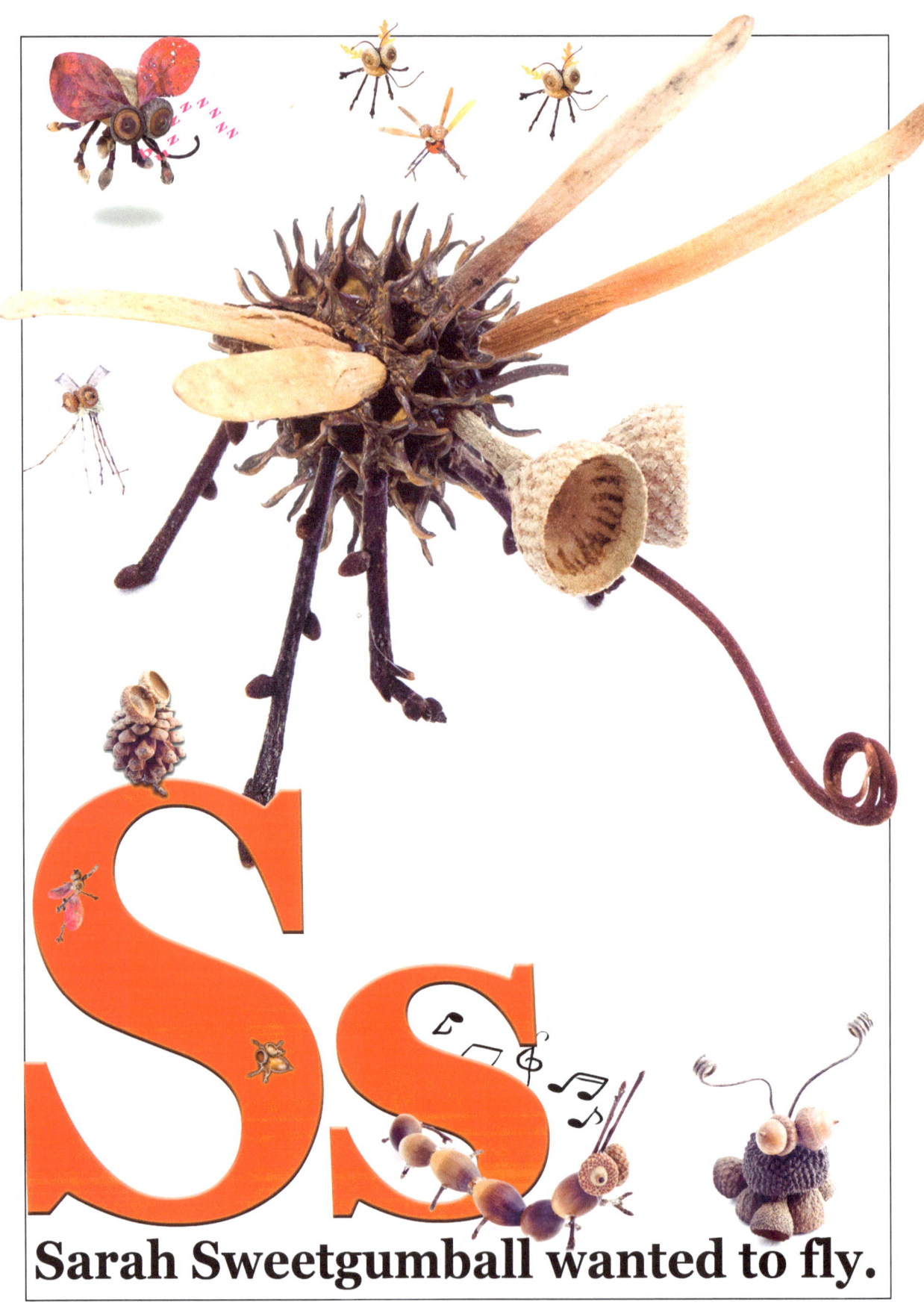

Sarah Sweetgumball wanted to fly.

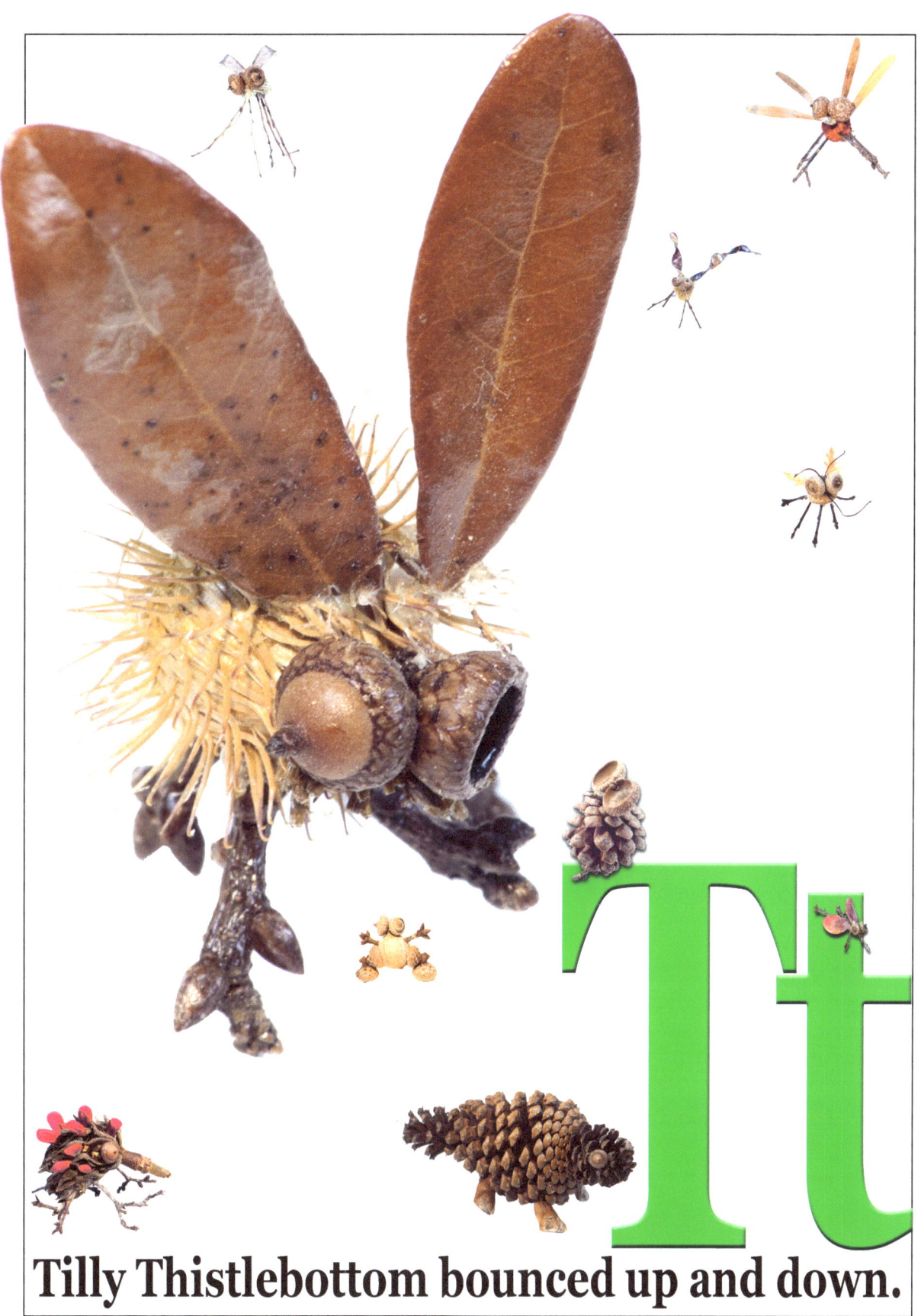

Tilly Thistlebottom bounced up and down.

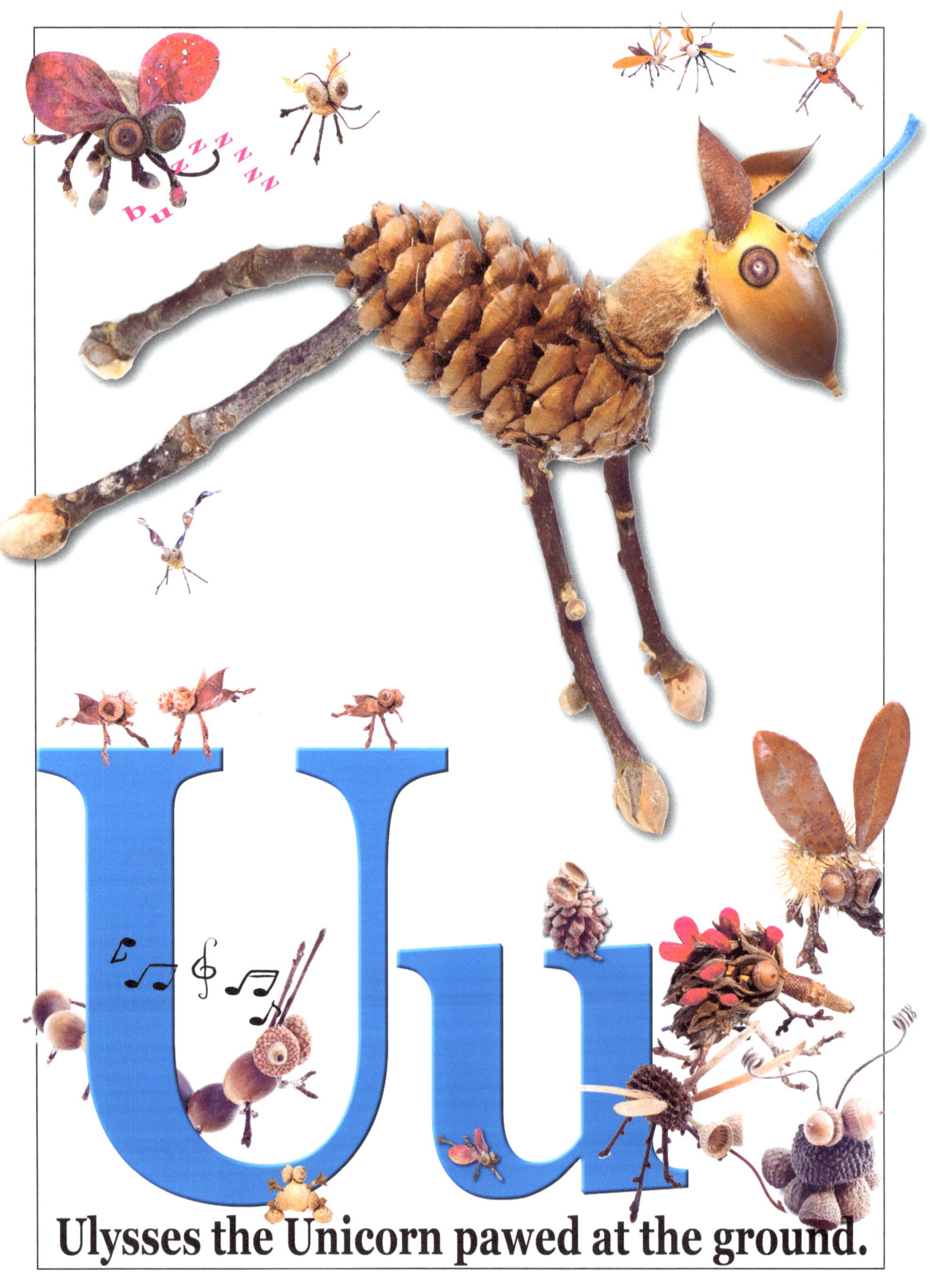

Ulysses the Unicorn pawed at the ground.

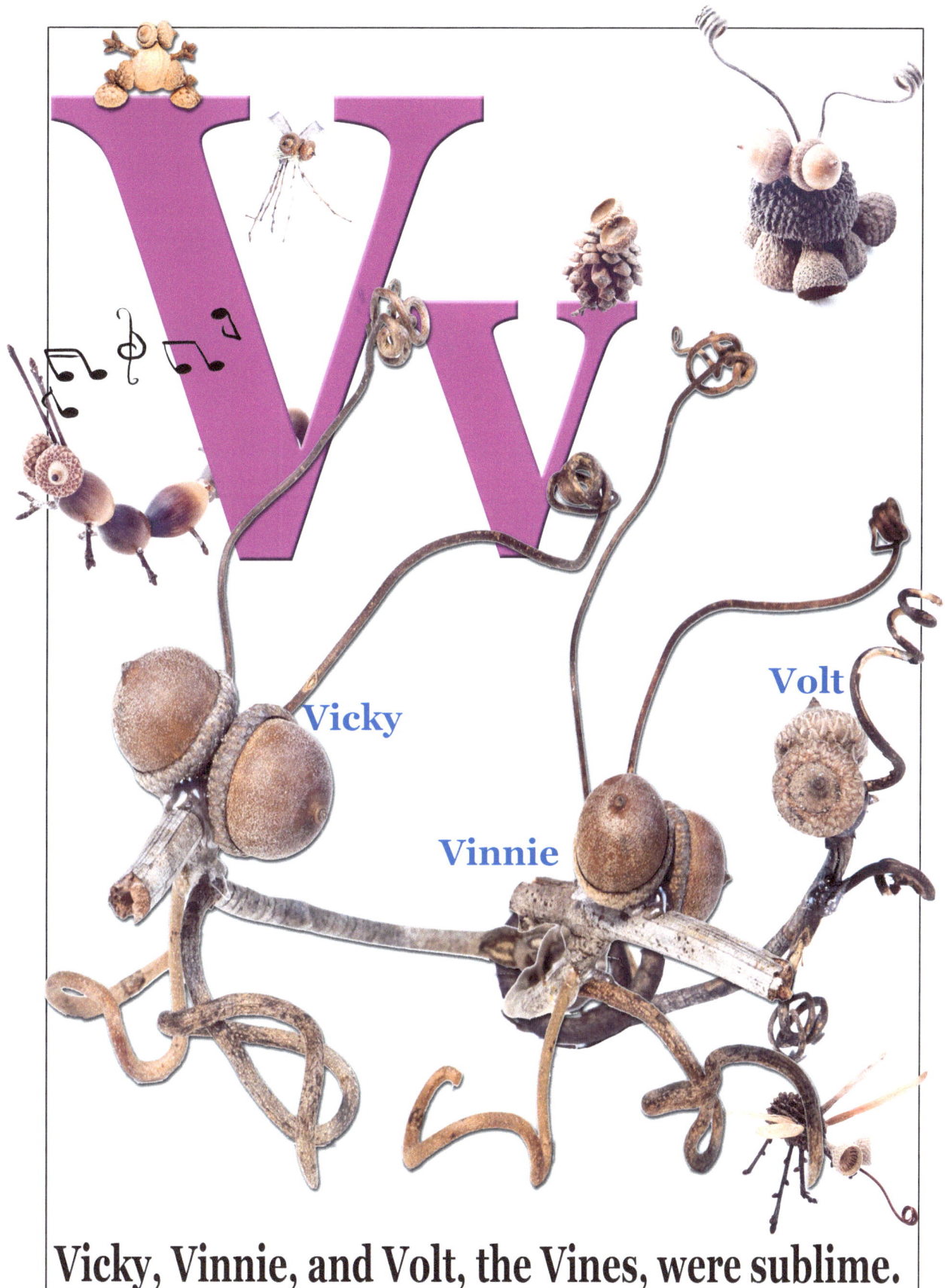

Vicky, Vinnie, and Volt, the Vines, were sublime.

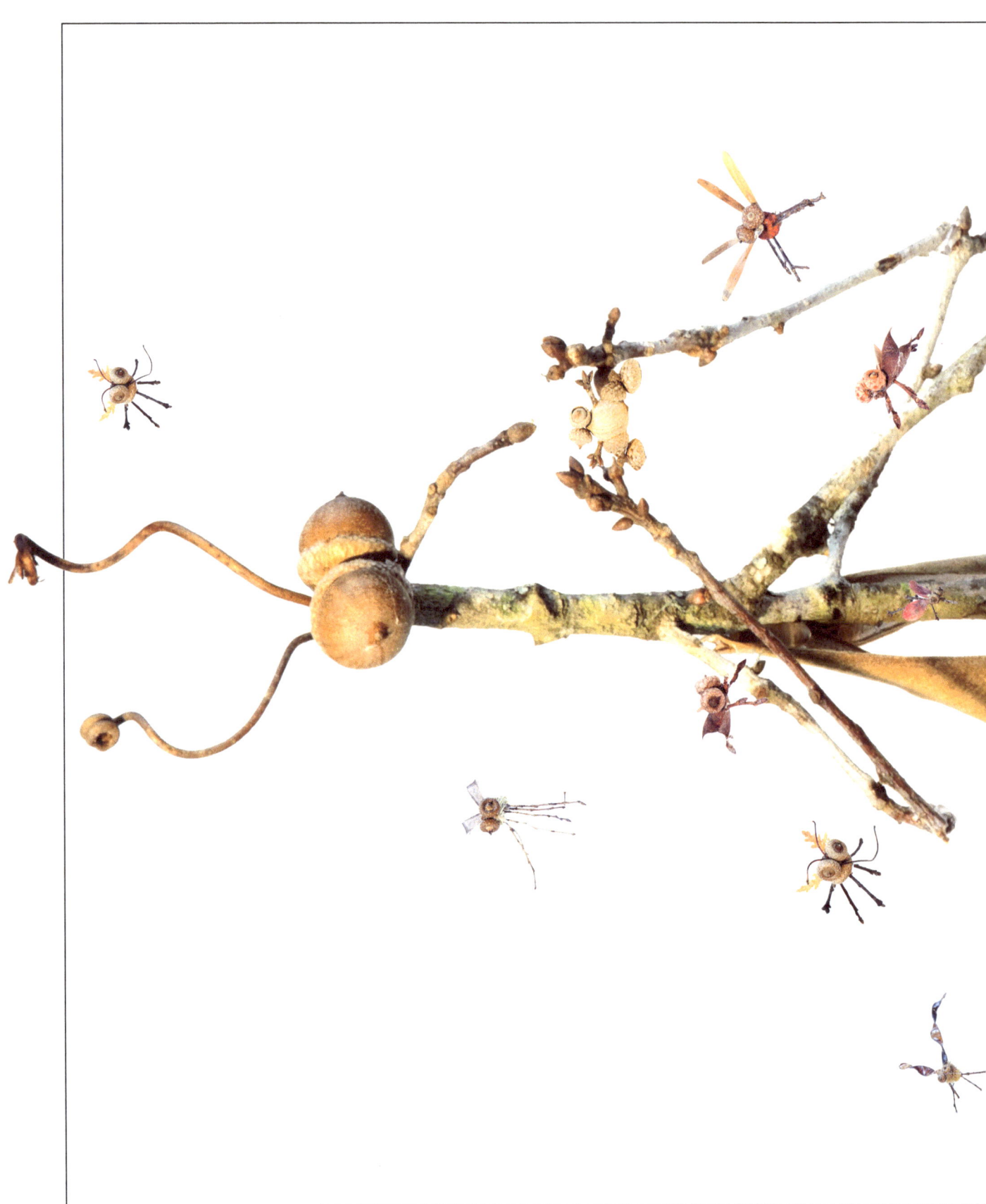

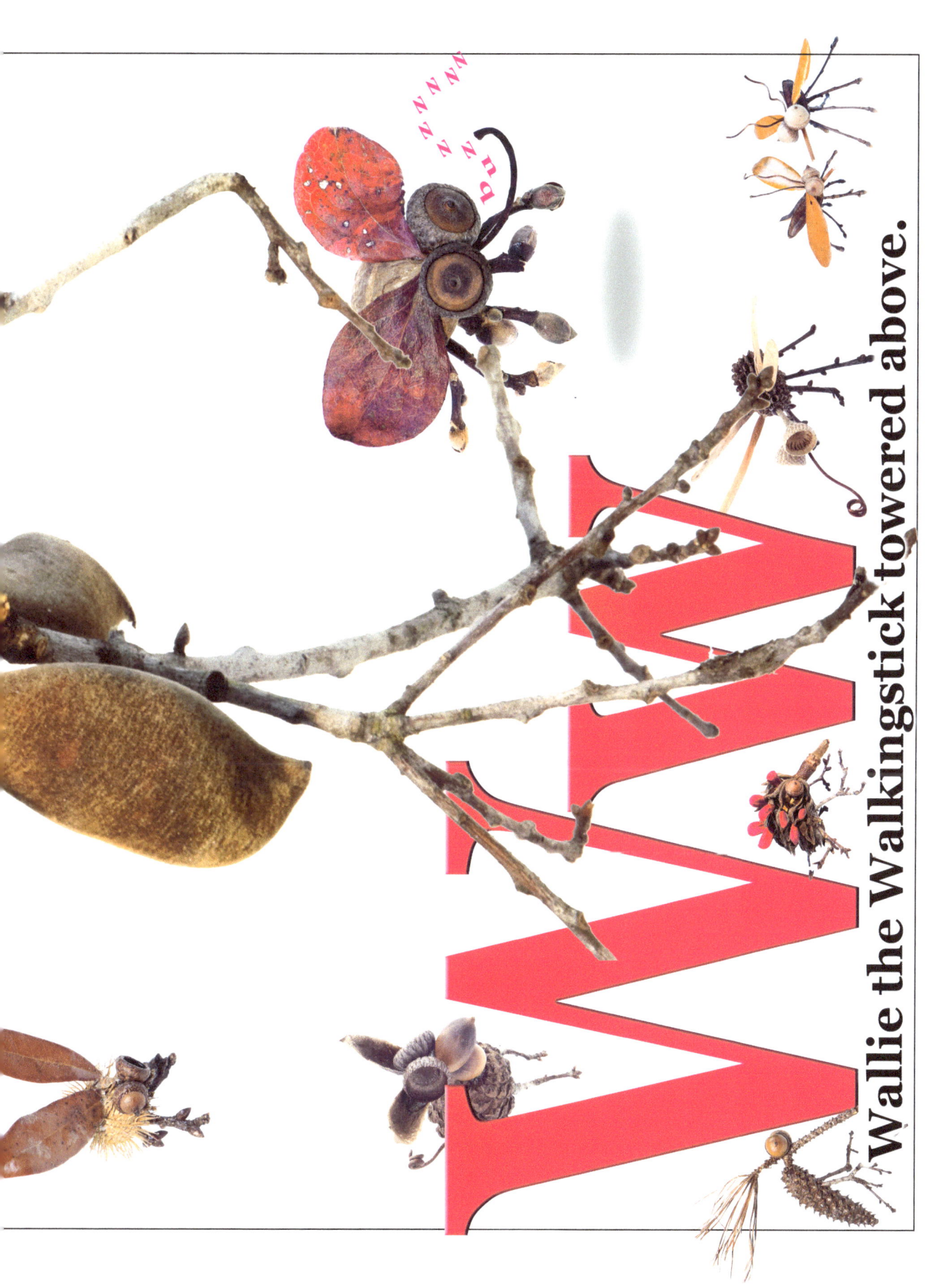

Wallie the Walkingstick towered above.

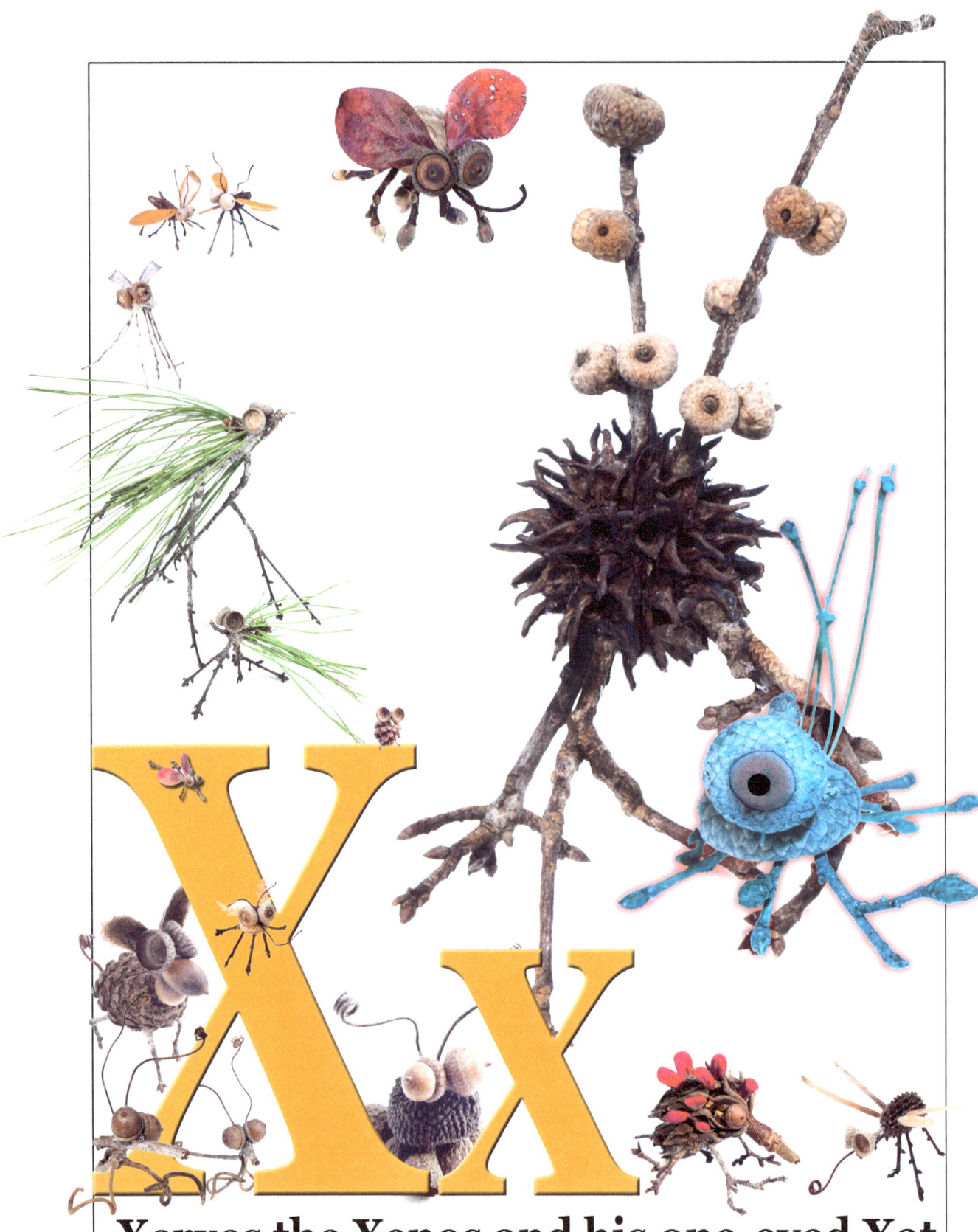

Xerxes the Xenos and his one-eyed Xat flew in from Mars or maybe the stars.

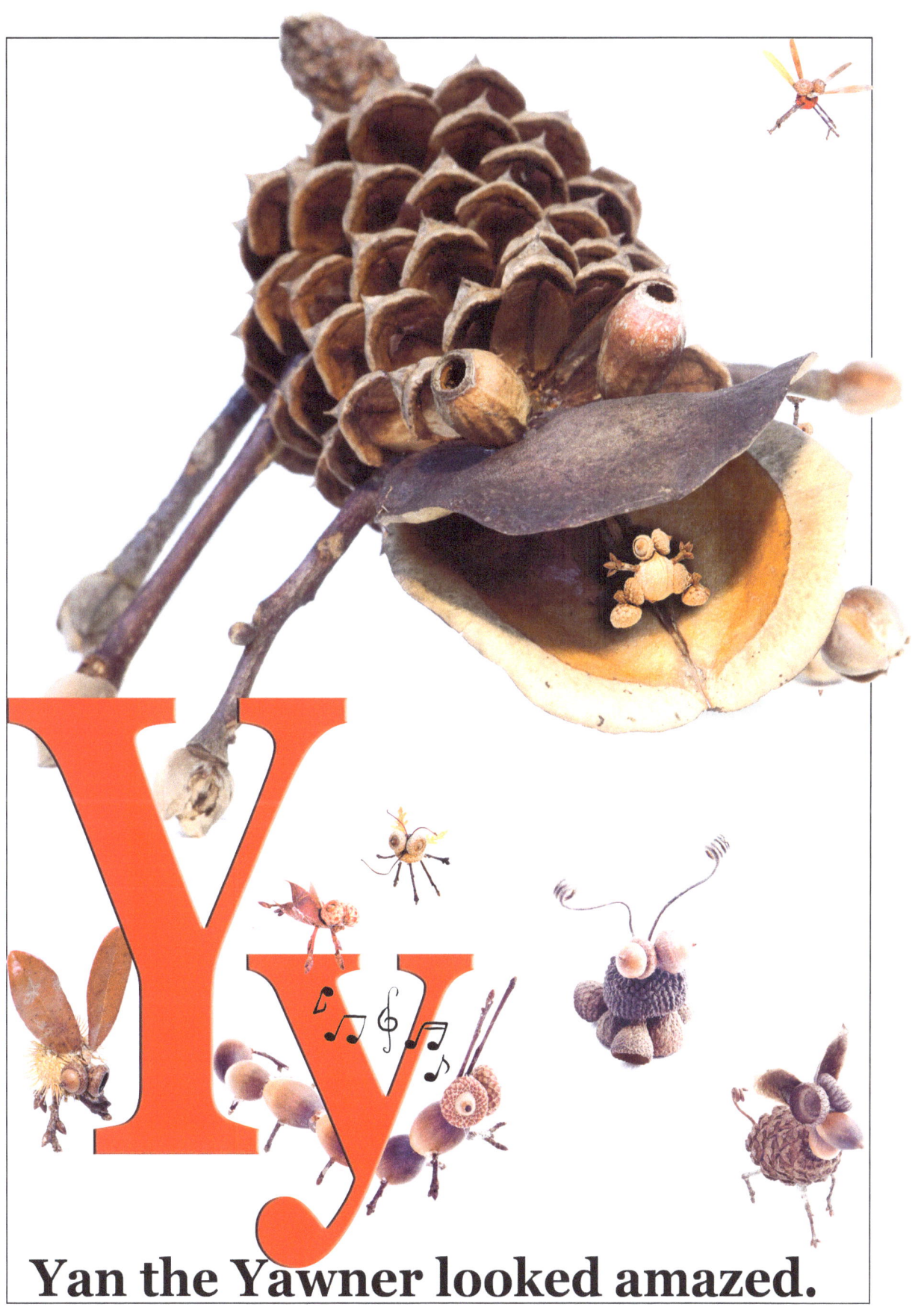

Yan the Yawner looked amazed.

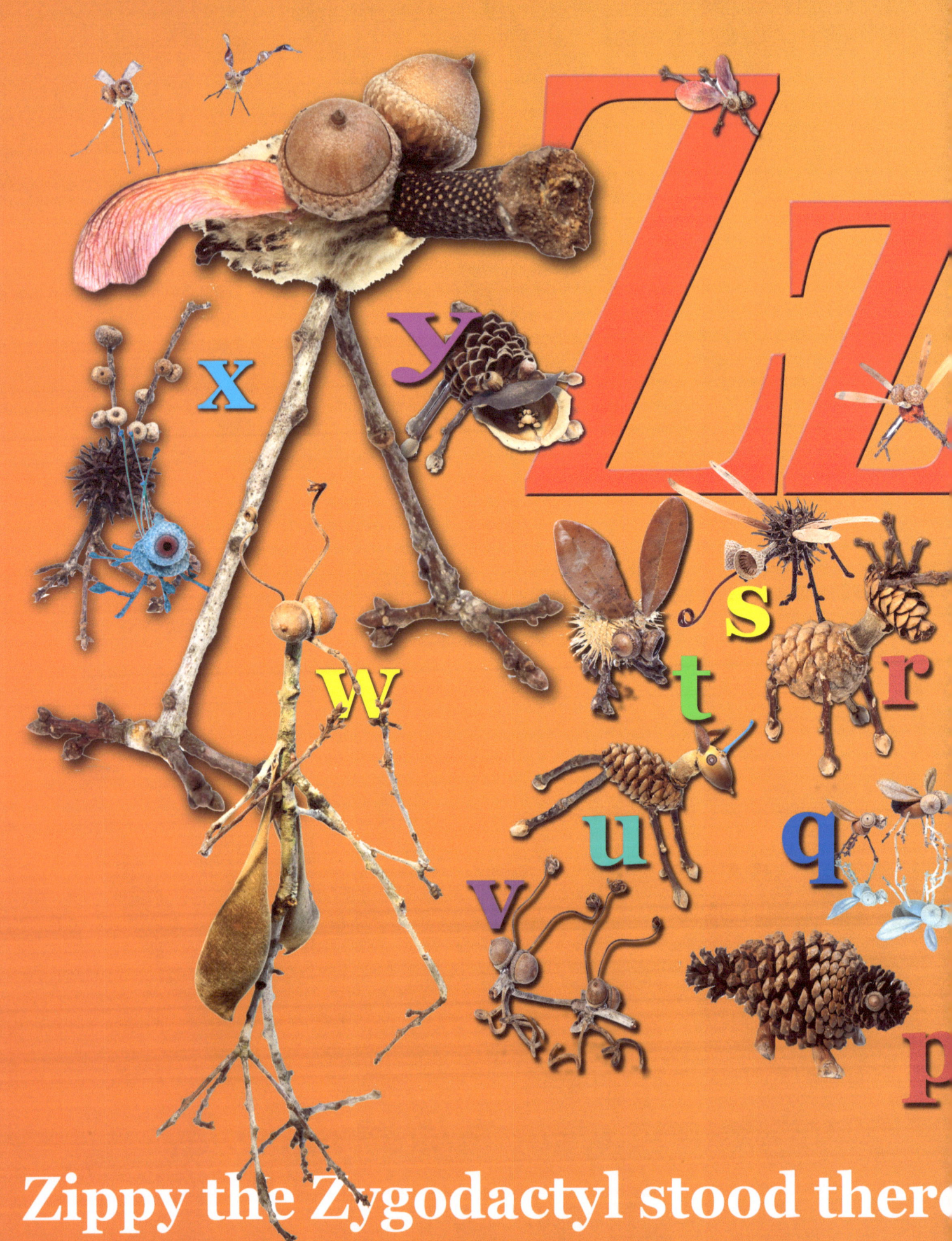

Zippy the Zygodactyl stood there

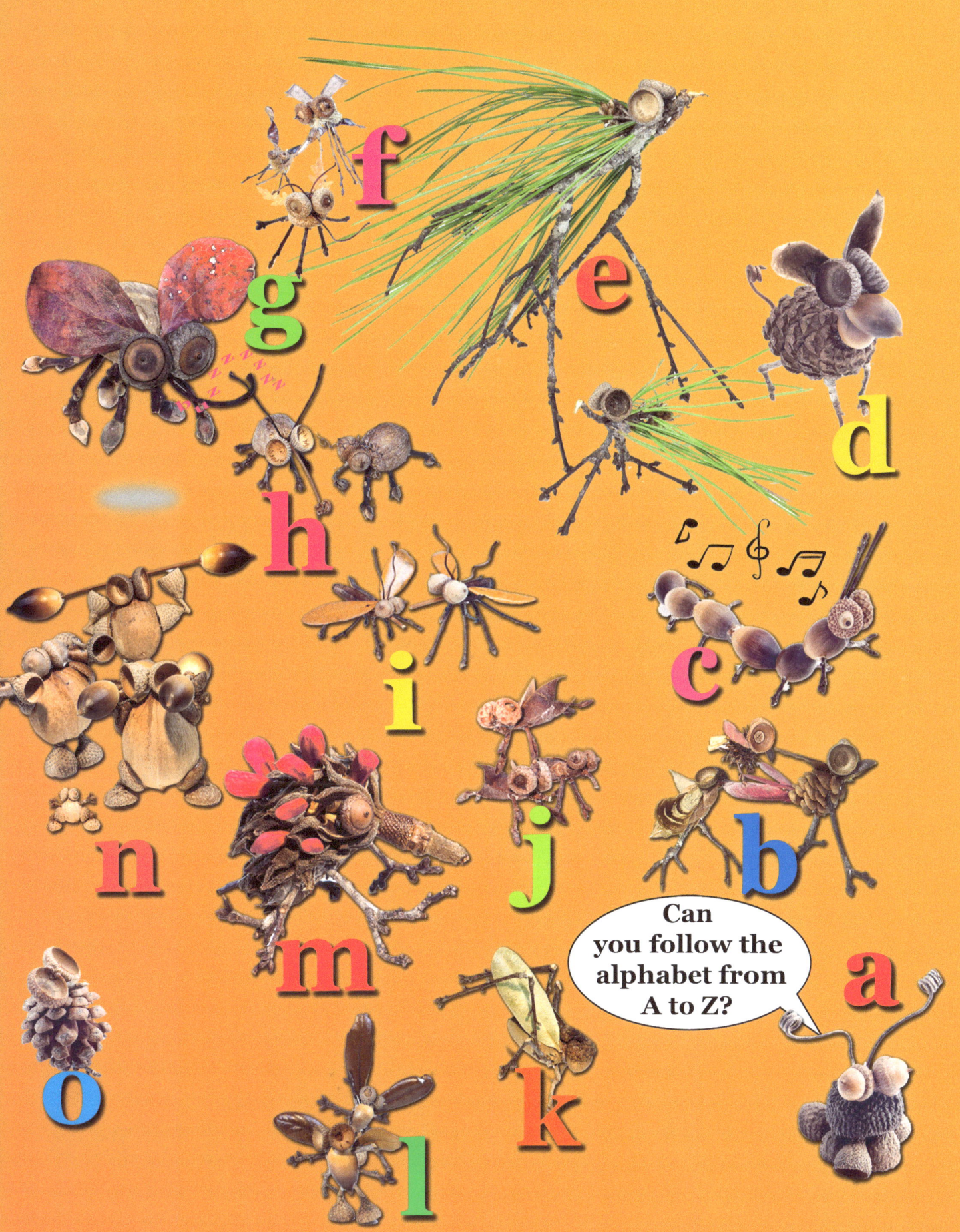

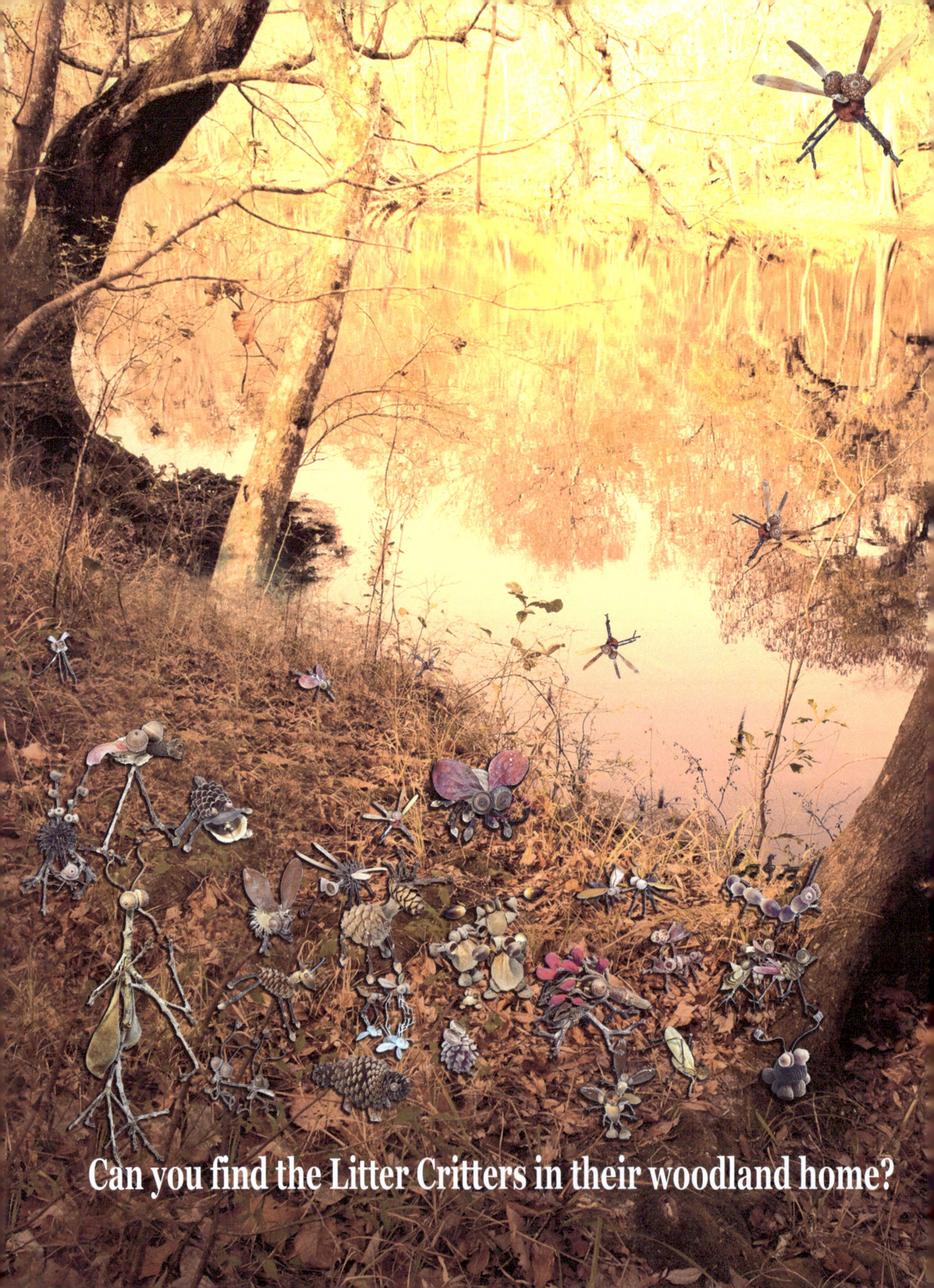
Can you find the Litter Critters in their woodland home?

NOTES

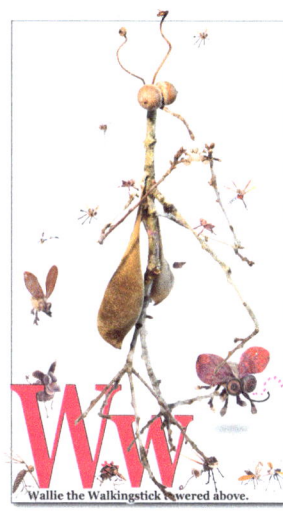
Wallie the Walkingstick towered above.

The Litter Critters live in the woodlands next to a shady river in north Florida.

All the Critters were created by Patience, who can't walk through any woodland without finding new friends hiding in the litter.

The beechnuts and iris pods are from Maine.

Magnolia cones have bright red seeds sticking out of them when they first fall.

There are six types, or flavors, of quarks in an atom which occur in pairs: up and down, strange and charm, bottom and top. Quercus is Latin for oak.

Unicorns do have blue horns.

Xenos means alien in Greek. It's a little known fact that aliens vacation along the shady river because they are small and don't like crowds.

Yan's yawn and eyes are from underneath two different trees in California.

Zygodactylic means two toes pointing forward and two pointing back.

Find a Litter Critter in a woods near you!

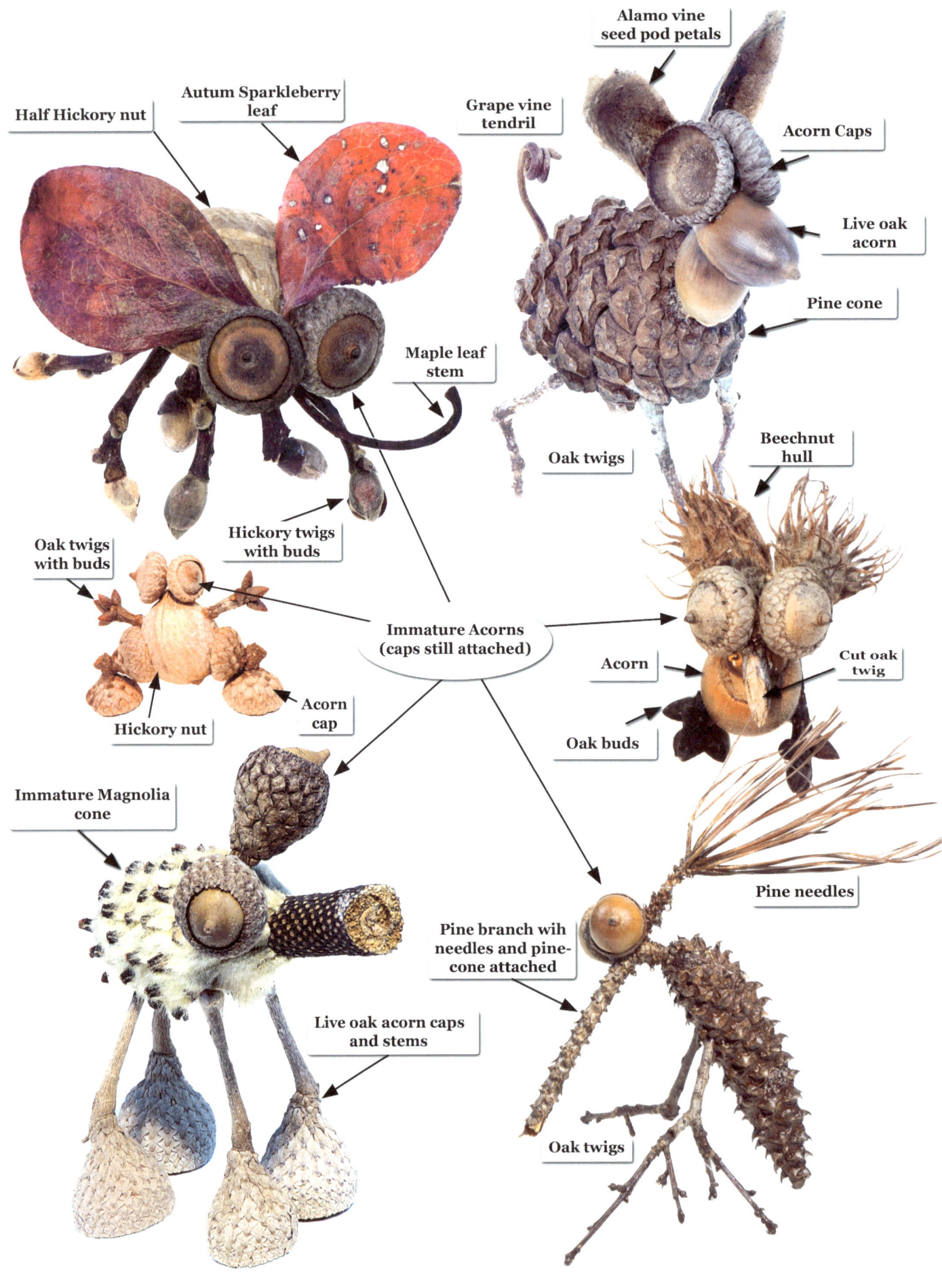

www.ingramcontent.com/pod-product-compliance
Lightning Source LLC
Chambersburg PA
CBHW041936240526
45473CB00034B/1731